BILINGUAL CHILDREN

Families, Education, and Development

Ellen Bialystok

TBR Books
New York - Paris

TBR Books is a program of the Center for the Advancement of Languages, Education, and Communities. We publish researchers and practitioners who seek to engage diverse communities on topics related to education, languages, cultural history, and social initiatives.

CALEC - TBR Books
750 Lexington Avenue, 9th floor
New York, NY 10022
USA
www.calec.org | contact@calec.org
www.tbr-books.org | contact@tbr-books.org

Photo Credit: Paola Scattolon Photography
Cover Design: Nathalie Charles

ISBN 978-1-63607-189-3 (paperback)
ISBN 978-1-63607-207-4 (hardcover)
ISBN 978-1-63607-351-4 (ebook)

Library of Congress Control Number: 2022943110

Table of Contents

Preface

With the expansion of multilingualism worldwide, many people are beginning to wonder how it impacts children. What a good question! Multilingualism is established through different paths, at different ages, and for different purposes, but the experiences and abilities it provides us always influence our cognitive, social, and emotional lives. Since we are now able to control our language learning experiences and opportunities to greater degree than previously possible, it is essential to pause and examine what we know about bilingualism, biliteracy, bilingual education, and their effects on our children, but also on aging individuals, and families in general. The global and historical prevalence of these skills should be reassuring to those who struggle with decisions about language use at home, at school, and in the communities. The purpose of *Bilingual Children: Families, Education, and Development* by Dr. Ellen Bialystok is to examine what is known about these issues from the scientific perspective, and explain it, so that decision-makers may choose what is best for everyone's well-being.

This book is a major review of the critical issues affecting multilingual families and a resource for parents as well as the professionals with whom they have a direct relationship, including teachers and clinicians. It provides an overview of what we know about the effect of bilingualism on brain development and academic achievement; offers practical suggestions for practitioners; and puts the related discussions in context by tracing major advances in the research on this topic since the 1980s. This text delves into how our language learning experiences impact, among other things, cognitive development, literacy acquisition, emotional skills, long-term health; and mental flexibility, meaning the adaptability to novel situations or changing social circumstances.

Dr. Ellen Bialystok is a well-known professor in the Psychology and Neuroscience Departments at York University, and the best-suited authority to guide us through complex topics such as language environment, cross-linguistic transfer, metalinguistic awareness, cognitive development, and biliteracy. She presents bilingualism from a developmental perspective and discusses its implications for education, cognitive development, mental health, and psychosocial identity formation.

Multilingualism is a gift. It helps us learn new things faster and take part in cross-cultural communication. It is also a skill that can be acquired and benefit us at any age. It is not just for children: multilingual adults are better problem solvers too! This book seeks to explain the science behind bilingualism, and what it does for people's minds and bodies. It will change for good how you think about knowing and learning languages, and it will provide you with insights as to why bilingual people are unique. It will be of great value to anyone who wants to learn more about bilingualism specifically, and multilingualism in general. As such, it fits perfectly with the Center for the Advancement of Languages, Education, and Communities' mission to promote bilingualism, empower multilingual families, and foster cross-cultural understanding while establishing language as a critical life skill, through the development and implementation of bilingual education programs that promote diversity, reduce inequality, and help to provide quality education while creating vibrant multilingual communities.

Fabrice Jaumont, PhD
President of the Center for the Advancement of Languages,
Education, and Communities (CALEC)

Acknowledgments

It started with a walk in Central Park. Fabrice Jaumont had invited me to New York to give some talks to people involved with bilingual education and the general community about my research on bilingualism. I have worked as a research scientist for over 40 years and my usual audience has typically been other academic researchers. However, over the years I have received emails from people who found me on the internet as an "expert in bilingualism" to ask my advice about how to organize languages in their homes – what to speak to their children, how many languages to include, what to do when their children refused to speak, and so on. These emails had been increasing in frequency, and it became clear that there were a set of common issues that all parents were concerned about. I answered all the emails, although with disclaimers like "There is no right answer" and "I'm not a clinician"; I just wasn't sure that anything I knew was useful. At the same time, I began receiving invitations from bilingual schools around the world asking me to speak to their teacher and parent communities to explain what we know about bilingualism. I realized that the information that I had been accumulating in my cloistered academic world had implications for people's lives and I became more interested in being involved in that translation from basic research to real life. I also realized that people wanted that information so they could have another tool to help them make difficult decisions and good choices for their children. And on that beautiful spring day, as we walked through the park, Fabrice said: "Write a book about bilingualism for parents, educators, and the general public". And so, I did.

Research is a team sport and I have been fortunate to have had outstanding team members. My research has been conducted by undergraduate students learning how to ask questions and design experiments, graduate students creating interesting projects to make unique contributions to the field, and postdoctoral fellows who bring new ideas to the table and move the research to a higher plane. All this activity has been supported by volunteer lab assistants and research assistants with high-level technical skills. I have also had the privilege of collaborating with colleagues, both senior and junior, who in the best spirit of cooperation have pushed the work to new heights. I am grateful to all of you for sharing the incredible experience and thrill of scientific discovery. Some of these people have evolved into highly valued friends.

On the wall in the entrance to my lab, there is a map of the world. As people joined the lab, we always asked them to put a pin in the place they come from. The map is covered in pins!! The group who produced this research represents an enormous number of countries, languages, religions, ethnicities, and every measure of diversity. Not only is that appropriate – I think it was part of the secret sauce that produced this body of work. Research is expensive and these costs have been covered by grants from several major funding agencies. These include the Natural Sciences and Engineering Research Council of Canada, The Social Sciences and Humanities Research Council of Canada, the Canadian Institute for Health Research, the National Institutes of Health in the United States, as well as several more specialized agencies, such as the Alzheimer Society of Canada and the Canadian Language and Literacy Research Network. I thank all of them for supporting my research over the years. I send special thanks to my friend and colleague Professor Fergus Craik. Our collaboration over the past 20 years has enriched my research and I have learned much from our discussions. Gus also patiently read this entire manuscript and made helpful suggestions for how to make technical lab research more engaging and more accessible.

Writing a book takes one away from family and friends, turning the writer into a somewhat grumpy hermit. I was probably more grumpy than usual because I wrote this book during a pandemic in which much time was spent in isolated lockdown. Therefore, I am, as always, grateful for the tolerance, patience, and support of my husband Frank during this process. My extraordinary daughters, Sandra and Lauren, left home years ago so they did not contribute directly to this work, but they are at the heart of everything I do.

This book is dedicated to the four most amazing people in my life: Raphaël, Gabriel, Rebecca, and Naomi. You are all tied for first place!

Ellen Bialystok, OC, PhD, FRSC

Chapter 1
Families and Languages

"Happy families are all alike; every unhappy family is unhappy in its own way." Such was Tolstoy's ponderous description of the state of 19th century Russian society. His idea was that happiness rested on a "sameness" that made all those families interchangeable, in contrast to the diversity and unpredictability of unhappy families. And so it is with language: monolingual families are predictable; multilingual families are full of surprises and no two are alike. There are no implications for "happiness".

Multilingualism has always been a feature of human societies. The history of our species is marked by constant migration [1], a process that inevitably led to problems of communication as groups spread out from their traditional territory (albeit very slowly) and encountered new communities. Even now, multilingualism is a prevailing feature of life in traditional societies. Jared Diamond [2] reported that on a visit to New Guinea he spent time with a group of local Highlanders and asked them how many languages they spoke; the *minimum* number was 5. In the industrialized world, the massive amounts of immigration at the beginning of the 20th century saw the populations of entire regions and villages leave their homes throughout parts of Europe and elsewhere to relocate in the West in search of a better life. Learning a new language was part of the immigration deal and nobody thought much about it; it was simply what you had to do. And yet we marvel at the facility with which some individuals can learn to communicate in more than one language, and we assume that the success commonly observed by children is evidence of some superpower available only to the young. We micromanage our environments to avoid exposure to the complexities of another language. We never travel without Google Translate fully updated on our phones. For the same reasons, perhaps, we are suspicious of foreign language education in schools where courses and enrollments are currently declining in many countries. Overall, we have an ambivalent relation to foreign languages: in some contexts, a foreign language is considered a luxury that imparts high status when it is mastered; in other contexts, a foreign language is considered a burden carried by immigrants who struggle to assimilate into the new society. But these contradictory judgments are reactions to precisely the same phenomenon: the ability to speak a foreign language.

By some estimates, for more than half the global population multilingualism is a reality [3], in which case, monolingualism is the outlier! Multilingualism is achieved through different paths, at different ages, and for different purposes. But languages matter, and the experiences and abilities we acquire with languages impact our cognitive, social, and emotional lives. In a real sense, the languages we speak influence who we are, who we interact with, and how we react to the world. At the same time, we are now able to control our language learning experiences and opportunities to a greater degree than previously possible. Language learning apps for smartphones are a growth industry, streaming services provide subtitles in a range of languages, and newspapers sometimes offer their material in a variety of languages. Throughout these developments, global immigration resulting from both personal choice and political displacement is increasing, transforming many countries that had traditionally been homogeneous and monolingual into communities that are substantially more diverse.

For these reasons, we live in a world where multilingualism may be more widespread and more accessible than ever. It is a good time to examine what we know about multilingualism and its effects on individuals, especially children. The prevalence of multilingualism should be reassuring to those who struggle with decisions about language use in their families, but we still want to know that we are making the best decisions possible for our children that are informed by scientific evidence. The purpose of this book is to examine what is known about multilingualism to understand its impact on children.

Why families?

Families are the crucible in which individual humans grow and cultures develop. There are no limits on how "family" can be defined, no restrictions on the number of adults involved, or specifications about their sex or gender or their biological relation to the children, but because babies are born helpless, they must be cared for. The immediate people responsible for their care are their family. And for this to work, there must be communication, and therefore, language. The language can be spoken or signed, there can be one or more than one, but its presence is necessary.

The origins of language acquisition begin before birth. Unlike the other senses, such as sight or touch, hearing begins in the womb and is functional from about the sixth or seventh month of pregnancy, although the sounds are muffled. This means that fetuses have been listening to their mothers speak for several months before they are even born. In a compelling demonstration of this point, researchers played short audiotapes of English and Tagalog (an Austronesian language) to newborns shortly after birth. Babies prefer what is familiar, so they would probably be more interested in the languages that they recognized. The results were dramatic. The babies whose mothers had spoken only English during pregnancy strongly preferred the English tapes, but those whose mothers had spoken both English and Tagalog during pregnancy showed equal interest in both languages [4]. Although their hearing was not good enough to distinguish individual words or sounds, the patterns of speech and rhythm specific to each language were clearly detectable and remembered. In some sense, therefore, the baby's socialization into the family, including the language or languages they will speak, begins before birth.

Without early experience with human interaction and experience with language, children's development is severely damaged. A striking example of the devastating consequences of children being raised without adequate human contact and communication is detailed in a chilling account by researchers who were brought in to deal with a particular situation [5]. Following the collapse of the Romanian regime in 1989, many children were abandoned and taken in by institutional facilities across the country. These facilities, however, lacked adequate resources, so the children were largely deprived of basic human interaction and suffered from profound developmental impairments. The immediate remedy was to place them into foster care with families who interacted with them in "normal" ways. This family experience led to dramatic improvements in their development. The earlier the children were given the opportunity to be part of a family, the better their outcomes. Families do this naturally, although to different degrees, but it is reasonably guaranteed that they will interact with their children at home. And therefore, language will happen.

Defining "bilingual"

It would be unusual for someone to get through life with absolutely no exposure to or knowledge of another language. Experiences such as education, travel, or immigration, typically include encounters with other languages. For this reason, the notion of a pure "monolingual" may be rather rare. But how much exposure or knowledge is required before one can be considered to be "bilingual"? The question turns out to be complex.

Before we ask whether someone is bilingual, we need to agree on what counts as a language. We think of languages as spoken systems, but language can also be signed, such as American Sign Language, or even invented, such as the Nicaraguan Sign Language, a language that deaf children had to create to communicate with each other because there was no official sign language in Nicaragua. These sign languages include all the features of any language and are learned by children in similar ways [6].

Even considering only spoken languages, it is not always easy to decide what should count as one. Many of them include regional variations or dialects, as in the range of speech found throughout Italy and France. The language spoken at the geographic intersection of these countries is a bit like both but not exactly like either, as it is based on an old form of Provençal, itself a separate language. Other languages, called *creoles*, are a simplified mixture of two or more languages, such as Haitian creole which combines

French and African languages. Dialects and creoles are generally not written, a feature that accounts for some people not considering them actual languages. Sometimes, similarity is treated differently for different purposes. Dutch and Flemish, for example, are spoken in different countries, but they are essentially the same language with small differences in some words and sounds. Languages also differ in register, a feature that refers to the formal (usually written) and informal (generally spoken) expressions of language. This separation of register is called diglossia. Arabic, for example, is diglossic because there is a considerable difference between the written form, called Modern Standard Arabic, and the spoken versions. To further complicate matters, the spoken forms are regional and vary sometimes dramatically across countries. How many languages should we say a literate Arabic speaker knows?

Once we agree on what counts as a language, the next challenge is to decide how much mastery an individual needs of each language to be declared bilingual. Do we require complete fluency? Is literacy necessary? How about just being able to order a meal in a restaurant or navigate the streets of a foreign country? If the speech is marked by a foreign accent or frequent grammatical errors, does that change the decision about bilingualism? The answers are mired in individual assumptions, cultural preferences, and political bias.

For these reasons, the question "Are you bilingual?" is deceptively simple and may be impossible to answer, yet the response stands at the center of all that we know about the implications of bilingualism. For example, a large body of research has explored the possibility that bilingual experience impacts cognitive development and brain structure (see Chapter 5), but all those results may depend on what we mean by "bilingual".

Psychology research frequently compares outcomes from two groups to determine whether the difference between them affects some aspect of performance. Participants are assigned to one of the groups and then everyone is assessed with the same test or measurement. If the overall results from the two groups are different, then the conclusion is that something about membership in that group was responsible. But for any of this to work, it is crucial that the *only* relevant difference between individuals in each group is the factor under investigation. For example, imagine a study to investigate differences in toy preferences for 4-year-olds and 6-year-olds. The question might be motivated by a practical issue from a toy company that wants to market a new line of games and is interested in the target audience. Following the standard procedure, two groups of children could be assembled, one consisting of 4-year-olds and the other of 6-year-olds. All the children would be tested for their toy preferences. Children's responses would then be analyzed statistically to see if any observed differences were reliable or were simply due to chance variations. If the results passed these statistical tests, then the conclusion would be that 4-year-olds and 6-year-olds prefer different toys. However, if all the 4-year-olds were girls and all the 6-year-olds were boys, then nothing could be concluded no matter how convincing the statistical differences turned out to be. In this case, the child's sex is a "confound": a variable that is not part of the study but interferes with the outcome. No conclusions can be made from confounded designs because it is impossible to know which factor is responsible for the results, that is, whether it is the main experimental factor (age) or the confounded factor (sex).

This procedure for comparing groups is widely used in psychological research and, providing there are no confounding factors, is a reliable way to understand how groups might differ from each other. Using this approach, studies have compared 4-year-olds and 6-year-olds on a cognitive reasoning task and shown better performance by the older children [7]. In another study, younger and older adults were compared on a memory recall task, revealing better performance by younger adults [8]. Yet other investigations have compared men and women on a spatial processing task and reported that men outperformed women [9]. Similarly, musicians and non-musicians were compared on an auditory perception task with the finding that musicians have more acute auditory perception than non-musicians [10]. Because the criteria for group membership are clear and the task is related to a hypothesis about the difference between those groups, the results can be easily interpreted and used to support general statements about the group. Therefore, we can conclude from these studies that older children reason better than younger children, younger adults remember better than older adults, men process spatial information better than women, and musicians perceive auditory discriminations better than non-musicians. But unlike those individual differences, bilingualism is not a binary category.

To apply the standard method of comparing across groups to research in bilingualism would require agreeing on the criteria for group membership. As we saw above, these criteria are not obvious [11, 12]. However, the situation is even more problematic for much research in bilingualism because the decision about which group participants should be assigned to – the monolingual group or the bilingual group – is often made by the participants themselves. An example comes from a recent study that attempted to establish whether bilingualism impacts cognitive function, a question discussed in Chapter 5. The researchers evaluated results from thousands of participants who completed an online battery of cognitive tasks. They reported that there were no significant differences in test results between the monolingual and bilingual groups so they concluded that bilingualism has no effect on cognition [13]. But how were participants making the decision about which group they belonged to? The study asked them to answer only one question: "How many languages do you speak?" As we have seen, the question is laden with assumptions, including what counts as a "language" and what counts as "speak"? For this reason, it is unlikely that anything can be concluded from this study. Bilingualism is difficult to define, and bilingualism research is difficult to conduct, but despite the challenges described in this book, we have been able to learn a lot about bilingualism and the effects it does (and does not) have on children's development.

As a final point, there is little consensus on the terminology we should use to describe children being raised with more than one language. A great deal of the research on bilingualism and the development of bilingual children is conducted in the United States, a context that is unique in many ways. To a large extent, bilingual children in the United States are of Spanish background with a wide range of language experiences and abilities in Spanish, are primarily from low socioeconomic backgrounds, and struggle at school [14, 15]. These children are learning English and most likely being educated in this language, so their degree of bilingualism is largely determined by their progress in mastering it. They are referred to in the literature by an alphabet of designations, including English Language Learners (ELL), Dual Language Learners (DLL), Limited English Proficiency learners (LEP), Language Minority (LM), and English Only (EO). Notably, all these terms evaluate children's language proficiency assuming that English is the standard by which everyone else is judged. However, they reflect the specific context of Spanish-speaking children growing up in the United States and do not describe the broader situation of children who speak one language at home and another one at school or in the community. Outside the United States, children who speak a heritage language at home do not necessarily share those profiles regarding socioeconomic status or academic success. For this reason, researchers Luk and Kroll [15] have proposed the more neutral term "emerging bilinguals". This term makes no judgments about the value, status, or proficiency of the languages themselves. Instead, it designates a group of children who have been given the opportunity to learn more than one language with no presumption about the outcomes.

Families, environments, and cultures

Ask members of a multilingual family which language people use when speaking to each other. Some might tell you, "We always speak Portuguese (or Urdu, or Spanish, or Cantonese, or whatever) at home because the children hear English (or French, or Spanish, or whatever) at school and in the community". This is a common arrangement for families trying to maintain a heritage language while living in a community where the main language is different. Another might answer, "I only speak English and my husband only speaks Polish, and our children answer in the appropriate language to each of us". This arrangement follows the popular rule of One Parent One Language, which we will discuss below. Yet someone else, perhaps a more self-aware parent, might say, "We speak

Spanglish (or Frenglish, or Chinglish)", to acknowledge a certain level of linguistic chaos in the family.

These arrangements correspond to three contexts that researchers have proposed to describe how bilinguals use their languages in real life situations [16]. These contexts can also guide our understanding of how bilingual families might incorporate languages into the home. The first case, called "single language context", is the idea that every language has its place. This arrangement is the least confusing: when you are at home, you speak this language; when you are out, you speak that other language. This helps guarantee that children will develop reasonable proficiency in both languages. In the second case, called "dual language context", different languages are spoken to different individuals in the same home. Unlike the single language context, knowing where you are (home) is not enough information to guarantee the appropriate language is spoken because it is also necessary to pay attention to who is speaking. The final arrangement, called "dense code switching", is the situation in which all the family members can use both (or all) languages and switch freely between them. Visitors to these homes may be baffled by the linguistic smorgasbord they encounter.

Family life is never as simple as it seems, so there may be other arrangements as well. For example, in multigenerational homes where not only parents and their children live together, there may be additional rules about speaking to grandparents or extended family members, or situations in which it is only the children who are bilingual and serve as translators for their parents. There are also numerous anecdotes about parents insisting on speaking the heritage language at home, that is to say, on creating a single language context, but the children stubbornly persist in speaking the community language, turning their home into a dual language environment. These rules are constantly modified by the unique situation that each family faces. For example, it may be that only one parent speaks the heritage language, or the parents each bring a different heritage language, or the parents have weak or no competence in the community language, or any one of many other configurations, all of which make these rules oversimplifications at best. But the three contexts described earlier capture most family situations. How realistic are they? Are some better than others? How should families manage their languages?

Families provide security, safety, care, and happiness, and the glue that underlies all of them is communication. Communication, of course, takes place through language, so language is the tool by which families carry out their social functions. *However, language should not get in the way of communication.* The nurturing functions of families should not be diminished in order to create a sort of language classroom. Rules about what languages individuals must speak may make good pedagogical sense at school, but they do not make good communicative sense within the family. Communication is always primary.

Take the popular example of the One Parent One Language system. This strategy was first proposed by the French linguist, Jules Ronjat, who wanted to raise his son to speak both French and German, his wife's language [17]. He documented his son's bilingual progress, arguing strict adherence to the rules was needed. This approach is still promoted as an effective way to raise bilingual children [18]. The idea is that assigning each parent one of the target languages will simplify the bilingual environment by making it more predictable and will improve the outcomes. By using this system, the argument goes, children will hear enough of each language and have sufficient opportunity to use each of them for meaningful communication. Nice idea, but does it work?

The problem with this approach is that it pushes the boundaries of the principle stated above: Language should not get in the way of communication. What happens when the parents are speaking to each other and the child walks in? Do they switch languages? Are the rules abandoned when there are visitors in the home? How much "slippage" is allowed when there are words missing in the required language? Is it ok to substitute from the other language? And the question most baffling to me: What does the family speak around the dinner table? Despite its possible pedagogical virtue, there is something inherently unnatural about this approach, at least if it is strictly enforced.

But aside from these practical questions, is One Parent One Language the best way to ensure that children develop high levels of proficiency in two languages? Some research evidence shows it is not. There are many studies of this question, but one is notable for its large sample size. For her study, Belgian linguist Annick De Houwer [19] sent questionnaires to almost 20,000 families in a part of Belgium where the community language is Dutch. From this large survey she identified almost 2,000 families that were bilingual to some degree because they spoke one of 73 different languages at home in addition to Dutch. These families were then included in a study of how language was used at home, including estimates of children's proficiency in both Dutch and the other language. The question was to determine if there was any relation between how the languages were used at home and how bilingual the children were. Two results stand out. The first is that regardless of the language choices, language rules, and language use patterns in the home, all the children became highly proficient in Dutch. This is important because it means that parents do not need to worry about children learning the community language: they will learn it in school and through their social interactions. The second is that the families that followed the One Parent One Language rule did not produce children who were more proficient in the home language than did families who followed other configurations. Proficiency in the home language was simply tied to the *amount* of exposure to that language. It made no difference who the speaker was or what the rules of use happened to be. Since all the children learned the Dutch to a high level, the more the heritage language was used at home, the more proficient they became in that language. It's just a matter of quantity: No special rules are required to designate who must speak that language. This result leads to a simple and practical recommendation: Use the heritage language as much as possible at home and let the community take care of the other language.

One language, two languages, three languages, more?

"We only speak one language at home because we don't want to *confuse* our children." One hears this a lot. Protecting children is one of the universal instincts that motivate parents' decisions. As it will be explained in Chapter 5, in the first half of the 20th century most people believed that the use of two languages created "mental confusion" in children [20]. These ideas were prominent a long time ago, and unfortunately, despite the immense amount of contradicting research, they endure.

Multiple language environments are not "confusing" for children at all. Language learning is always different for children in different families, even monolingual ones. Some children are simply more "verbal" than others and learn language more quickly and more fully, but other factors in the home environment also impact this process. By far the most important of these is the socioeconomic status (SES). By 18 months old, babies in low SES families know substantially fewer words than children in higher SES contexts, a gap that increases with age [21] and is also evident in children learning two languages at home [22]. Some researchers have considered this problem to be so serious that it has been proposed that by the time they are 3 years old, children from the wealthiest families have heard 30 million more words than children from the poorest families, a difference called the Word Gap [23]. More recent analyses of those data come to a more modest conclusion: closer to 4 million words [24]. The claim remains controversial in that the numbers may be overestimated, but what is indisputable is that there are pervasive differences in children's family environments that can be traced to the impact of the SES on children's language learning.

The difference in language learning between high and low SES families is largely explained by the *amount* of language spoken in those contexts, with more exposure in high SES leading to richer vocabularies. However, the difference in language learning between monolingual and bilingual families is explained in terms of the *number* of languages. Obviously, the presence of more than one language is the defining feature of bilingual homes, but recall that the most important feature in determining bilingual language development is the amount of exposure children have to each language. Here the situation is no longer similar to SES. There is a limit on how much speech can take place in a single day, and if there are two languages spoken at home, then logically that speech must be divided between them.

Again, we are back to math. If a bilingual child hears about half as much of each language as a monolingual child, will that child not learn it as well as a monolingual, but only half as well? The answer is no! On average, a bilingual child will know fewer words in each language than a monolingual child who only speaks that language (discussion in Chapter 3), but there is much more to language acquisition than just accumulating words, although they are obviously important. Bilingual children also know words in another language, and they are very strategic about using all their resources to improve communication, even if it includes borrowing words from their other language. Of course, children's proficiency will develop more fully in the language to which they have greater exposure, so we are talking quantity again. However, there is no evidence that this vocabulary difference interferes with their ability to use language in complex ways, something that is more important than scores on a vocabulary test [25]. Research examining bilingual language acquisition has revealed important differences between individual children and different learning contexts, but the developmental milestones and trajectories are similar for children whether they are learning one language or more than one, a finding that should reassure parents [26].

In addition to learning two languages instead of one, bilingual children also must learn how to keep them separate, especially if both of them are spoken by both parents. How do they do this? The incredible finding is that even preverbal infants, those who do not speak yet, are able to distinguish between the two languages in their environment [4]. They can focus on the one being used without confusing it with the other one [27], and can detect when a speaker has switched languages just by watching a video with the sound switched off [28]. Beginning in infancy, before they have uttered a single word, these two languages are understood to be different systems, so there is no reason to expect they will cause confusion. In an odd extension of this idea, using magnetic resonance imaging (MRI) to record brain activation, it was recently shown that even dogs can tell the difference between languages and distinguish between the ones they have heard and those that are new [29]. I doubt there are any implications of these results for children's language learning, but if dogs can do it, perhaps we should be less surprised that humans can as well!

If we can be sure that children are not confused and that they can learn whatever languages are used at home, is there a limit on how many they can learn? There are many reasons that parents might want their children to learn three or more languages. Many families have multiple heritage languages, and it is normal for parents to want their children to connect to all those pieces. But is it a good idea? Is it even possible? The only restriction to the number of languages that children can learn is time, but it is a significant one. As we have seen, acquisition requires enough time to hear and practice the language. This is the main problem for children from low SES environments because less language is heard and used overall. Bilingual children typically have smaller vocabularies in each language than monolingual children who only speak that language, so adding more languages dilutes the time and resources even further. The math is simple: if the number of hours in a day is fixed, and the amount of interaction between children and parents is also reasonably constant, then dividing that time across more languages logically leaves less time for each. The prediction from the quantity principle is that less time will lead to less proficiency. None of this is to say that parents should *not* introduce as many languages as they like to their children, but rather that they should be realistic in their expectations for the outcomes.

A final point is to note how multiple languages are represented in the mind. This configuration is surprising and may explain much of the research on the effects of bilingualism that will be discussed in this book. If I were to build a brain into which I could store knowledge of two (or more) languages, I would probably give each one its own compartment and install a switch to signal which one is being used in the moment. That way there would be no confusion: when I was speaking French, the switch would be positioned to French and no interference from English could get in the way.

However, there is no language switch [30]! All the languages a bilingual speaker knows are jointly active in the brain (although not in consciousness) when that person uses any one of them. This seems risky because it should be easy to slip and produce the wrong language, but bilinguals rarely do. The usual explanation for how bilinguals avoid such intrusions is that they engage general attention mechanisms to focus on the language they need. These general attention processes are part of the executive function (discussed in Chapter 5) and because of their constant use in language selection, those processes become modified through extensive use for bilinguals.

Revisiting bilingual families

Out of the immense variation that defines bilingual families, a few simple commonalities emerge. First, regardless of the rules or patterns of language use in bilingual homes, children will learn both languages, although not to the same level. Typically, the community language will become dominant, especially as children go to school and socialize in that language, and proficiency in the home language will depend on the quantity and quality of the opportunities for learning and using it. Second, details of the home environment, including SES, parental education, presence of siblings, quantity of adult-child verbal interaction, presence or absence of literacy, among other factors, impact children's bilingual language development in predictable ways.

There is yet another dimension that has not been discussed. Bilingual families are often bicultural families, and language is the key to unlocking that part of the child's life. In some cases, entire rituals, central to the families' beliefs and identity, require some competence in another language. In other cases, the presence of grandparents or other extended family members requires basic communication ability from the children, but the reward is access to different cultures and worldviews that are part of the child's heritage. Children are learning much more than just language, and the cultural knowledge that is part of a bilingual home is just as important to their development as the language that conveys that culture. In an interesting proposal for how bilingual babies separate the two languages in their environment, Padmapriya Kandhadai and her colleagues [31] suggest that part of the process may rely on cultural information, leading to what they call "cultural binding". Languages are often associated with such cultural features as ethnicity, food, music, and so on, and by noticing these associations, children may be supported in their ability to distinguish between the speech systems in their environment.

Bilingual families are certainly not all alike, and they meet the inevitable challenges they face in different ways, but they share similar outcomes, namely, children learn the languages of the home and the language of the community. There are of course countless anecdotes of children entering a period of rebellion in which they refuse to speak the home language because they find it embarrassing to be different from their assimilated peers, but generational clashes such as these exist beyond any dispute about language; it is in children's nature to object to their parents! The challenges, however, are rewarded in the long run as families learn to accept, adapt, and adjust to the journey.

Take-away conclusions

- Communication in the family, in any language, is the mechanism for children's language acquisition and overall development
- The amount of the home language that children hear and use is the most important factor in how well they learn it
- Children in multilingual families understand the difference between the languages from infancy and are not confused by the presence of several of them

Chapter 2
Time and Timing for Becoming Bilingual

Stop any random person on the street and ask them: "Who learns languages better, children or adults?" If they look somewhat mystified it is likely because they think the answer is too easy to even bother asking: "Children do, of course!" They may even back up the answer with a personal anecdote or some maxim of general wisdom like, "Children absorb languages like sponges", and possibly wonder how you could not know something so obvious. But as with most simple questions, there are landmines of complexity lying just below the surface and the answer is never obvious.

The simple question about age glosses over a wide range of factors: First language or second language? Learned naturally or in a classroom? With or without literacy? For what purpose? And so on. Yet these details that make language learning situations different from each other are all lumped together under the single heading of age, on the assumption that differences in learning that come with it are so large that no other factor needs to be considered. And although age is important, the usual explanations for this effect are simply not supported by evidence.

Why should age matter?

The belief that age is the most important factor in determining language outcomes derives from a concept called the "critical period". This notion, central to a variety of developmental and biological achievements, is that a particular experience must take place within a specific maturational time window for an important developmental outcome to occur.

The most famous example of a critical period comes from the animal world in the form of "imprinting". There is a window of time during which newly hatched birds and some newly born mammals become attached to their mother and as a result, follow her everywhere. This attachment is called imprinting. Imprinting turns out to be a good arrangement: as long as the babies are close, the mother will feed and protect them, increasing their chances to survive and thrive. This is an old idea that was understood in some form for several hundred years, but it was refined and popularized by Konrad Lorenz [32] who demonstrated that imprinting in geese chicks took place between 13 and 16 hours after hatching. Lorenz even showed that he could make new chicks imprint on him instead of on their mothers by being the first thing they saw during that critical period window, an outcome made famous by photographs of him walking through a field, followed by a line of geese. It turns out, however, that it was actually Lorenz's yellow boots they imprinted on and nothing about himself. Nonetheless, the chicks did attach themselves to something other than their mother that showed up at just the right time.

The demonstration provided a clear example of how a biologically constrained period guaranteed a development that was essential to survival, in this case, attachment to the mother. This early work with geese chicks provided an important model for future studies of critical periods that tied development to biological conditions. Critical periods are innate constraints and so demonstrate the powerful role of innate factors on future outcomes, including those in human development. However, as we will see in Chapter 3 in a discussion of early views of intelligence, science is sometimes intertwined with politics, and notions of innate characteristics of species are easily abused. Lorenz achieved widespread eminence for his work and won the Nobel Prize for Medicine in 1973, but his ideas about innate behavior and their role in group selection were used to support his commitment to the eugenics policies of the Nazi party to which he had belonged. Following World War II, he renounced his party membership. However, those eugenicist views relied on an outsized role for innate forces on behavior, a point to which he devoted much of his research. It is impossible to know whether his politics shaped his science or the other way around, but they were clearly intertwined.

Whether or not Lorenz misused the concept for his own purposes, his research confirmed that critical periods in some form are central to development, including human development. For example, several critical periods have been identified for visual development and show that visual experience is required during specific time windows after birth for the child to develop normal visual perception [33]. Some infants are born with dense cataracts that obstruct patterned light, so the world appears as a blur. Until recently, many of these children were not treated immediately, and this created a period during which they were deprived of visual experience. Research following these children over many years showed that there was a window of time after birth during which the cataracts needed to be removed for vision to develop normally. If that did not happen, the early deprivation of sight led to abnormal visual perception throughout life. Fortunately, these cataracts are now detected early, often at the time of birth, and a relatively simple intervention removes them, so vision is immediately restored. This example is a clear case of a critical period because it is essential for the baby to have visual experience in the immediate months after birth for visual processing to develop normally.

But is there a critical period for language learning? Language is part of the complex cognitive world. It does not belong to the perceptual world like vision, or to the physical world like the following response of the geese chicks for imprinting. No one claimed that the chicks had any conscious or even unconscious experience of attaching to their mother; only that they were programmed to follow the first thing they saw move within the critical period after hatching. We think of language as one of the defining features that make us human, and we acknowledge that, in some way and to some level, all humans learn language. If there were a critical period for learning language during which some essential experience needed to take place, would there be a risk of excluding some individuals from this fundamentally human ability? The question about a critical period for language acquisition has enormous consequences.

First learn a language

Before we can address the question about a possible critical period for language learning, we must make a distinction between learning one language, any language, and learning additional languages beyond that first one, even if multiple languages are learned at the same time. In other words, is there a time limit just for getting some language in place? The claim from a critical period approach is that exposure to language is required within a specified time for normal development to occur. However, once there is a language, it is possible that the system can then support additional languages regardless of when they are learned.

The idea may be logical, but it is incredibly difficult to test whether there is a critical period for first language acquisition. The gold standard for research design uses randomized control trials in which individuals are randomly assigned to conditions, different treatments are given to the groups, and outcomes of the groups are compared. This is the method used in clinical drug trials in which one group receives the drug and another receives a placebo. If the design has been carefully constructed, better health outcomes from the drug group suggest that the drug is effective in treating that condition and the next steps would be to obtain approvals and market the drug. It is unlikely that University Ethics Boards will approve a study that requires randomly assigning newborn babies to "language" and "no language" groups! However, there are some natural circumstances in which children are deprived of language exposure early in life, a situation that creates the necessary conditions to test the role of a critical period in first language acquisition in a somewhat experimental way.

There are a handful of extreme cases of children who were deprived of language input due to abuse, neglect, or medical limitations. The most famous of these is the case of Genie, a child who was essentially locked in a room between the ages of about 18 months and 13 years old [34]. Once she was discovered in 1970, she received the attention of the best psycholinguists at the time with the intention of teaching her language and restoring some quality of life to her. She was also seen as the "test case" that would resolve the question of whether a first language could be acquired after a critical period. Despite years of instruction and therapy, Genie never learned much language. However, the extreme abuse and extraordinary circumstances of her childhood make it impossible to conclude anything about the role of a biological critical period in her devastating story. In fact, the tragic situation was never a good test for the critical period hypothesis because Genie did have language exposure until 18 months, and that is likely past the close of the critical period in any case.

A more benign natural experiment comes from studying children who are born deaf to hearing parents, and therefore, do not get any language input until the condition is discovered and they are able to interact with, and learn from speakers of a sign language, such as American Sign Language (ASL). ASL has all the features of any other natural language, including phonology, vocabulary, grammar, and so on, but is conveyed visually through sign rather than orally through speech. Rachel Mayberry and her colleagues have been studying the acquisition of ASL for many years [35] and have produced compelling evidence showing that whether or not there are critical periods in establishing a first language, there are clearly age-related effects on this development. She tested adults who had been born deaf and assessed how proficient or native-like their ASL was in terms of when they began to learn it. People who began learning ASL in the first two years of life developed proficiency in the language that was similar to that of native speakers for whom ASL was introduced from birth. Typically, this early exposure happens when the parents are also deaf and ASL is their first (and possibly only) language. However, individuals for whom the initial exposure was delayed because they did not have the opportunity to interact with the ASL community until later in childhood, never developed ASL skills to the level of native speakers, and sadly, since this was their only language, never developed native-like control of any language. Similar results were reported by Elissa Newport [36], who compared proficiency in ASL for deaf adults who were first exposed to sign language at birth, early in life (4 to 6 years old), or later (after 12 years old). As with the research by Mayberry, the results revealed better mastery of ASL by earlier learners, and incomplete mastery by the oldest learners. These patterns are consistent with a critical period for learning a first language.

The idea that there is a biologically determined critical period for first language acquisition has also been explored in terms of the neural, perceptual, and cognitive components necessary for language acquisition. Janet Werker and Takao Hensch [37] describe the biological developments in the brain in the first two years of life needed to identify and distinguish among the sounds and patterns that provide the basis for language learning. These abilities are then traced to specific critical periods that have clear onset and offset windows and, in many cases, known biological bases. Therefore, Werker and Hensch argue that in the first two years there are multiple critical periods in which the underlying mechanisms for learning a language are established. Initiating language learning after that time, for example, after children are 2 years old, will not lead to typical and complete acquisition of language because of the missed biological maturation. Their conclusion is that in the first two years of life there are biological windows that create the conditions for first language learning.

And then add more

There is good evidence that learning a language of any kind needs to be achieved within a biological window of development, sometime in the first two years of life. But once a person knows *some* language, do biological pressures continue to restrict when it is best or even possible to learn another one? This is the idea behind the claim that children learn languages better than adults. The argument is that there is a privileged time for learning additional languages, just as there is for learning a first one, and that learning beyond that time will not be as successful. This view extends the critical period idea to second languages. Alternatively, does knowing one language set the language mechanism in place so that additional languages can simply be grafted on to it at any time? What is the evidence to decide between these possibilities?

Unlike tests for a critical period for first language acquisition, the question applied to second languages does not require ripping infants away from their parents and randomly assigning them to language environments, as there is plenty of natural variation in exposure to a second language that can be studied. Yet, there is a strong bias to consider that the problem has already been solved and conclude that the reason why second-language learning is, apparently, more difficult for adults than for children, is because of a critical period for second language acquisition.

The explanation that (first) language acquisition relies on a critical period can be traced to the seminal work of American linguist and neurologist Eric Lenneberg [38], who was the first researcher to study the brain basis of language learning. However, the extension of this idea to a second language and the durability of that belief may rest on a misreading of Lenneberg's important work [39]. He was the first theorist to take a biological approach to language by connecting aspects of language acquisition to brain function and exploring the connections between language and cognitive systems. However, his claims about second-language acquisition were more confusing. He claimed on the one hand that languages learned after puberty would inevitably be marked by a foreign accent, and that they could not be learned automatically by mere exposure, as a first language can. However, he also argued that because languages are all fundamentally similar to each other, the "matrix for language skills is present", suggesting that the foundation for second language learning is provided by having a first language. The first two observations are demonstrably correct – second languages learned later in childhood are rarely acquired through simple immersion and foreign accents are a frequent feature, but the third point is more troubling. If the "matrix for language" is present by virtue of having a first language, then something besides a critical period must be responsible for the imperfections in second-language mastery. Although the "matrix" may not be biological, it is a template on which languages are acquired. Lenneberg's work is generally used to support the presence of a critical period for second-language learning that ends around puberty.

Looking at the evidence

The term "critical period" is a technical concept, so if we conclude that a particular development is controlled by a critical period, its defining features must be present. Two of these features are (a) clear boundaries that define the window of the period, particularly its close, and (b) evidence that learning inside that window is somehow different from learning outside of it. The evidence for acquiring a first language during the first two years of life meet these requirements, and therefore supports the conclusion that there is a critical period. For second-language acquisition, the evidence is much less convincing.

Consider first the boundaries. In the research with baby geese, Konrad Lorenz was clear that imprinting needed to take place between 13 and 16 hours after hatching; outside that period, no effective attachment was formed. For first language acquisition, researchers Werker and Hensch [37] identified multiple components that needed to be established within the first two years of life, each within its own defined time window. For example, the organization of the component sounds that make up the language being learned is fixed around the 10th month, closing the window on how the sound system can be modified. But what are the boundaries that define the close of a critical period for second-language acquisition? Researchers have offered various answers, including 5 years old [40], 6 years old [41], 12 years old [38], 15 years old [42], and 17 years old [43]. Which is it?

The second feature is that the outcome of learning that takes place within the critical period must be fundamentally different from the learning outcomes if it takes place after the close of the critical period. In other words, differences between learning inside and outside the critical period should not simply be small differences in proficiency but must be qualitatively different from each other, either in the types of mastery shown or the processes used during acquisition. But studies comparing second-language outcomes to age of acquisition of the language generally find a continuous relation between the age of second-language acquisition and proficiency in that language, with no cut-off to separate qualitatively different outcomes.

Most of the research investigating this question compares the language proficiency of people who learned a second language at different ages to see if their test scores differ. That was the approach taken in the influential study by Jacqueline Johnson and Elissa Newport [42]. They gave an English grammar test to 46 individuals who had immigrated to the United States at different times in their lives. Their assumption was that the age of immigration marked the age at which English learning began, an assumption that may or may not be correct for all participants. The question, therefore, was whether scores on this grammar test were related to the age at which the individuals began learning English. Recall that evidence for a critical period needs to show a clear for the window that marks the end of successful learning and qualitatively different outcomes inside and outside the critical period. Based on the test scores, they concluded that there was a critical period that ended at 15 years, after which second-language learning was unreliable. Their results are shown in Figure 1.

There are several things to notice in this graph. First, the test is out of a maximum of 270, but average scores never dip below 210, which is not terrible performance; as a test score it is 78%, which is not bad. Using a small scale for the graph (specifically, the scale on the vertical axis) exaggerates apparent differences between the scores. Second, despite their interpretation that the critical period ends at 15, it seems that the most abrupt change happens at around 7. Finally, the sample size in this study was quite small, and the test score differences among children in each group were very large. This combination of a small number of study participants and a lot of variation in scores makes conclusions unreliable.

Ellen Bialystok

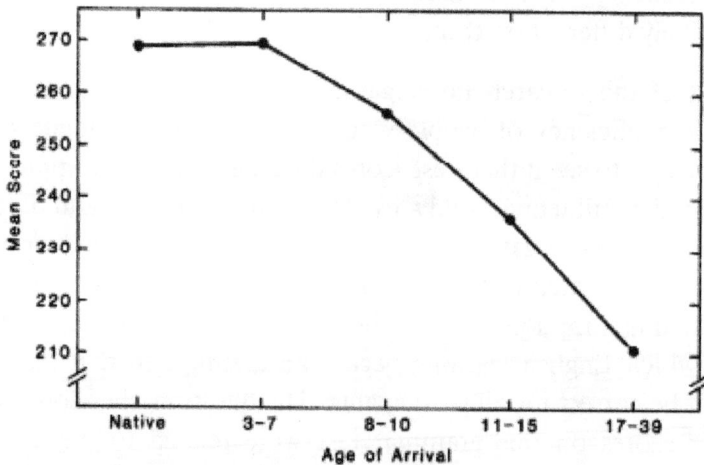

Figure 1. Results from Johnson and Newport [42] showing relation between age of arrival and score on English grammaticality judgment test. Reprinted from Johnson and Newport [42].

More typically in this type of research, groups of individuals who are designated as "early learners" or "late learners" are compared for differences in ultimate proficiency, usually based on a test score. But the results from this approach are not consistent: Similar studies of groups of early and late language learners have produced different results, although younger learners generally achieved more than older learners without any consensus on the defining points for "younger" or "older" [44].

In experimental research, there is always a trade-off between *control* and *generalizability*. Both are needed to make any conclusions about the study results. Control refers to the researcher's ability to make sure participants in the study are equivalent on all measures except for the one relevant to the research question. Therefore, in a study of the impact of early or late second-language learning, except for the age at which they started learning the language, early and late learners must be similar in all respects: age, education, sex, socioeconomic status, and whatever else might be relevant. This need for rigorous assessment means that the sample sizes for these studies are inevitably small, as in the 46 people who participated in the Johnson and Newport study. But if we are so careful about controlling all those features of the participants, then how can we be sure that the sample is representative of a larger population and that the results will apply to a new group that may differ in some of those features? This is the problem of generalizability. How large and how diverse can the sample be and still allow adequate control yet permit generalizability? There are statistical procedures for calculating the optimal sample size prior to conducting the study that conforms to principles of power and reliability. Such calculations may put this ideal size at around 100 or 200 participants, considerably more than the sample used in most of these studies, and often beyond the resources available to researchers to conduct an individual study.

But what if we sacrifice control and dive head-first into generalizability? In this case, the approach would be to test an extremely large number of participants without much concern for controlling the details that make the individuals different from each other. If the sample size is large enough, those details should simply average out across groups. This is the approach taken by my colleagues and me in a study that examined this question using census data [45]. In 2000, the United States census included questions about language learning and proficiency for the first time. These were the questions asked to respondents: when did they arrive in the U.S., what country they arrived from, and how would they rate their proficiency in English? Because the form also included their birth date, a simple calculation is needed to determine their age at their time of arrival in the U.S. The census also collected other demographic information, such as the amount of formal education they had received. The question for our study, therefore, was whether there was any relation between their age of arrival and their self-reported proficiency in English. There are enormous problems with using these data as evidence for the question: we have no idea whether they already knew English before they arrived but, like Johnson and Newport, we assumed that immigration marks the beginning of English language learning. More seriously perhaps, there is no independent and objective measure of the reliability of their self-rating of English proficiency: we only have their word. These are serious limitations, but they are offset by the sheer weight of the data. Our analysis included 324,444 speakers of Chinese and 2,016,317 speakers of Spanish.

The results from this enormous sample were simple. There was essentially no difference between the results for the Chinese and Spanish groups, even though the Spanish group was almost seven times larger. The results are shown in Figure 2, plotted separately for each language group, but the patterns are obviously similar. Age of arrival is plotted along the horizontal axis with older ages further to the right, and self-rating of English is on the vertical axis with better ratings higher on the scale. The relation between these two variables is simple: as age gets higher, the self-reported score for English proficiency declines. That is entirely expected. However, three features of these curves rule out an explanation of the decline in terms of a critical period. The first is that there is no break in the curve, that is, no visible evidence that there is a cut-off beyond which something fundamentally changes about proficiency outcomes. As we saw earlier, specifying a close to the critical period is essential to its definition. Second, the proficiency curve is similar throughout —it gradually declines as age of arrival increases— so there is no evidence for qualitatively different learning mechanisms inside and outside a supposed critical period. Third, the data are plotted in the figure as five different lines for each graph that separates the respondents by their highest level of formal education. In both graphs, these education lines are perfectly ordered in that more education is associated with higher proficiency even though all the lines follow a similar declining slope as age of arrival increases. But more importantly, the gaps between these education lines are larger than the gaps between consecutive ages of arrival. Education is more important than age in determining success in mastering a second language. No interpretation of the critical period can account for that finding.

The evidence described so far has focused on the degree of proficiency achieved in the second language. But the critical period argues as well that the processes by which the language is acquired must be qualitatively different inside and outside the critical period. This is a more difficult question to evaluate. However, a comprehensive review of neuroimaging studies of second language learning that occurred inside and outside a supposed critical period reveals no qualitative differences in the brain mechanisms used to learn the language or the neurological processes involved in that learning [46]. In short, the essential features that are necessary to conclude that second-language learning is the product of a biologically determined critical period have not been met.

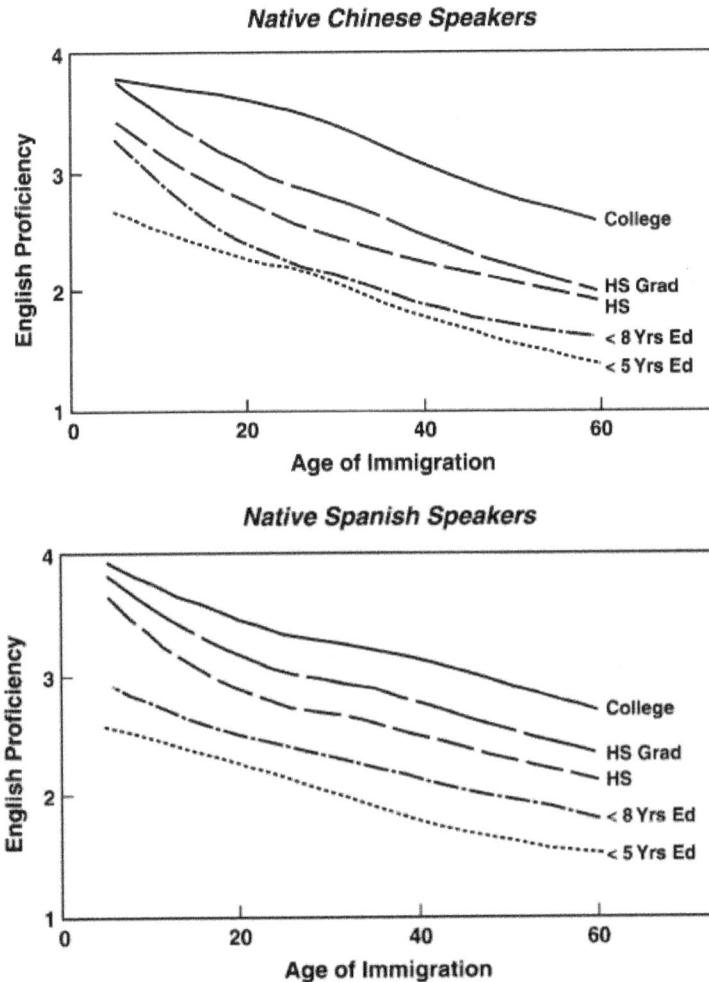

Figure 2: English proficiency by age of immigration for (A) Chinese speakers, N = 324,444 and (B) Spanish speakers, N = 2,016,317 [45].

Ellen Bialystok

Are children better language learners?

Many years ago, Catherine Snow, an eminent developmental psychologist who studies language acquisition, was living in the Netherlands and was struck by how often people told her (ignoring the small detail that she was an expert in language acquisition) how amazing it was that children learned a second language better than adults. Being an inveterate researcher, she decided to do a study. Unlike previous research, she and her Dutch collaborator [47] followed a group of English-speaking participants for one year who were between 3-years old and adults when the study began and documented their progress in learning Dutch. Surprisingly, by the end of the year, the best learning outcomes in virtually every category tested were found in the 12- to 15-year-olds, a group that is past the close of the critical period in most accounts; the slowest learning was found for the youngest group, 3- to 5-year-olds.

Why is the belief in a critical period for second-language acquisition so persistent, despite little supporting evidence and no agreement on what the relevant time frame for such a critical period actually is? Studies offered in support of the idea of a critical period continue to be produced. In one large-scale study by Joshua Hartshorne and colleagues, more than 600,000 participants completed an English grammar test on-line and the results were analyzed through computational modeling to determine learning rate, learning trajectory, and so on [43]. The results were similar to those in the study by Kenji Hakuta and colleagues. [45] (Figure 2) except that the oldest learners in this case were 30 rather than 60. Yet, despite this continuous declining curve, the authors argued that there was an abrupt break at 17 (much like Johnson and Newport's claim for 15) and concluded that 17 marks the close of the critical period. The authors state at the beginning of the paper that they were not following any theoretical interpretation of "critical period", an odd concession for a technical term. Once the strict definition of the term is dismissed, it is illogical to argue that they have found evidence for a critical period and that it ends at 17. Instead, their study fits well with other research showing that there are strong age-related differences in the outcomes of second-language learning, but that these effects are gradual and do not follow the restrictions imposed by a biological critical period. In a reanalysis of Hartshorne's data, Frans van der Slik and colleagues [48] attributed most of the effects reported by the former to the effect of schooling. At the very least, factors in addition to age are relevant in determining the outcomes of second-language learning.

One reason it is hard to give up on the idea that there is a critical period for second-language acquisition is because the anecdotal evidence is very compelling: on average, young people, especially children, appear to master a second language more easily than adults, and languages learned earlier in life generally reach higher levels of proficiency. Paul Krugman, a Nobel laureate economist, talks about "zombie economic theories" [49]. These are ideas that have no empirical support but are deeply embedded into the mainstream political culture and seem unshakable. One example he uses is "trickle-down economics": the idea that supporting the rich through such measures as tax cuts will encourage them to increase spending in their businesses, creating opportunity and wealth for the poor. It has never happened, yet it remains the primary justification for economic policies favoring the rich. In some sense, the idea that there is a critical period for second-language acquisition is a zombie theory – it is impervious to evidence.

There are reasons for the observed age-related differences in second language learning achievement that have nothing to do with a critical period. Life is different when one is 6 years old, 15 years old, and 30 years old, and those differences have an enormous impact on the outcomes of second-language learning. Think of all the ways that language learning is different for children and for adults. During the first few years, learning language is the main job of children, and the adults around them join forces to help: they speak slowly and clearly using colorful intonation, talking about things that are in the child's view, choosing topics of interest, and repeating as necessary. Sentences begin with simple structures that become more complex as the adult believes the child is ready to move forward. How many adults get this kind of attention? If an adult is immersed in an environment where there is a new language to learn, the language is likely to be spoken rapidly, or at least at normal pace, concerned with abstract topics, and based on complex grammar. Unlike children, who are likely to be praised for any reasonable utterance, adults try to make themselves understood and succeed when some meaning has been transmitted. Not many adults will be praised for saying "More juice" or "Look, doggie"! Children's experience with language acquisition is completely different from that of adults' in that it includes support and motivation to continue through the difficult early phases, and the acknowledgement of success for the simplest achievements.

The situations in which people of different ages find themselves as they attempt to learn a second language impact how successful the learning will be. Being immersed in the language is better than having only classroom study, having opportunities for practice and use is better than being isolated, and having the time, motivation, and resources to devote to effort is better than trying to squeeze language learning into the other demands of real life. In the study conducted by Snow and Hoefnagel-Hohle, the children went to school and were immersed in Dutch, but adults went to work, opened bank accounts, and managed life for the family. The 12- to 15-year-olds group had the best of all worlds: school, friends, immersion, and no responsibility.

But what about the persistent foreign accent that marks older leaners? Is this evidence of a critical period? Although it is undeniably more difficult to achieve native-like pronunciation with greater age, this too does not meet the standards for a critical period. There is no clear age or change in trajectory that marks the point beyond which a foreign accent will be present. Also, accent is different from the rest of language, the way you speak is deeply connected to your identity, and social, emotional, and cognitive changes that take place around puberty can make it difficult to present yourself to the world in a new way.

By ruling out a biological critical period for second-language acquisition, the alternative is that languages can be learned at any time. They will not be learned with the same ease or to the same level of success, and the age at which second-language learning begins is an enormous factor in determining these outcomes. But native-like proficiency, including native-like accents, is not excluded. The mere existence of individuals who achieve these levels – and there are many such people – means that the problem is not in our stars but in ourselves.

Take-away conclusions

- Biological conditions that take place on a specific timetable are likely necessary for the establishment of a first language, meeting the criteria for a critical period
- Second-language acquisition, in contrast, appears to become more difficult as age increases, but the criteria for a critical period are not met
- Many factors contribute to how easily or how well a second language is learned, and age is an important one, but there is no evidence of a biological limit on learning a second language.

Chapter 3
Educating Bilingual Children

For as long as there has been immigration, there has been bilingual education. But nobody called it that. It was not designed by curriculum consultants, linguists did not weigh in on ideal approaches to language pedagogy, and no one paid attention to what was happening: children of immigrants simply went to school along with the other neighborhood children and were educated (or not) through a language that was different from the one they spoke at home. At the same time, but from the opposite perspective, bilingual education was embraced by elite classes to provide privilege: children of the pre-Revolutionary Russian bourgeoisie were educated in French among other languages [50]. Whatever the origins, bilingual education is now a flourishing option, and the subject of substantial research in education, linguistics, and cognitive psychology. What is bilingual education and why has it catapulted to a position of such prominence in education circles?

Bilingual education is an umbrella term for a range of programs that have been designed for an even wider range of children and a host of special circumstances. Broadly speaking, bilingual education refers to any school program in which more than one language is used to teach academic content or any situation in which the language of schooling does not match the language of the home or community. In short, these are programs in which children are exposed to new languages because they are the instructional language in school. The reasons for incorporating the languages, the specific languages chosen, the structure of the program, and the relation between the school languages, the community languages, and the home languages vary, and these details influence educational outcomes. Ofelia Garcia and Heather Woodley [51] offer an excellent review of the varieties of bilingual education that explains the social, political, and linguistic context for the various programs.

Overriding these details about specific programs is the distinction between "bilingual education" and the "education of bilingual children." These concepts are not the same, and each brings its own goals and problems to be solved. For bilingual education, the focus is on designing an educational curriculum to develop bilingual (or multilingual) competence in children by using a language other than that of the community (or home) as the medium of instruction. One example of this arrangement is the popular French Immersion programs that were developed in Canada to teach high levels of French proficiency to anglophone school children. For the education of bilingual children, the focus is on teaching the community language to those who are already bilingual, usually because the community language is not the language used at home. Sometimes the home language is used as a temporary means of transitioning children to the community language, as is the case for transitional bilingual education programs for Spanish-speaking students in the United States. However, the education of bilingual children also describes the education of those for whom no special curriculum adjustments are made. For example, children who speak Mandarin at home, but attend school in an English-speaking community; children who speak Arabic at home but attend school in a French-speaking community; and children who speak Greek at home but attend school in a German-speaking community are all cases in which bilingual children are being educated through a language that is not used at home. The majority of research focuses on the first case, where instruction through a non-home language is offered in school, but those studies can help us understand what happens in the second case, when children who are already bilingual attend school in the community language.

Politics is always part of educational decisions – education policy is a thriving subfield within education studies – but the insertion of politics into bilingual education is especially noticeable. In the United States, bilingual education has been a controversial topic almost since the founding of the nation, and from the beginning these discussions were deeply political [52]. There were legal restrictions against using any language except English in American schools, but after several test cases, those restrictions were ultimately challenged in the Supreme Court in 1923. This court case led to a ruling that overturned the prohibition on the grounds that it violated the constitutional guarantee for individual rights [53]. Eventually, the Bilingual Education Act of 1968 recognized the needs of minority children with limited proficiency in English to have fair access to education and created funding for programs that would assist these children so they could succeed in American schools. The act specifically noted that these children needed to develop proficiency in both English and their home language. The act was largely focused on Spanish speakers, but subsequent groups, such as Chinese speakers, introduced amendments to the act to expand its scope. The Supreme Court ruling of Lau vs. Nichols in 1974 guaranteed the rights of minority communities to educate children in non-English languages in American schools.

Bilingual education has gained enormous attention and has increased in popularity in recent years, but the main purpose and preferred structure for this educational program are still disputed. Bilingual education is used both as a means of instilling bilingual language proficiency in children who are essentially monolingual, and as a scaffold for integrating immigrant children into the community culture. These two goals correspond to the two concepts distinguished above: bilingual education and the education of bilingual children. There is now a reasonable body of research that has evaluated the efficacy of programs that serve both goals.

Succeeding in bilingual education

Parents want their children to succeed in school, a desire that is both universal and profound. For that reason, decisions to place them in an educational program that introduces a new language are taken seriously. Although research does not directly answer many of the questions that parents entertain, there is a body of evidence that addresses the main issues.

The primary goal of early schooling is to establish the skills upon which children will build their educational futures, and the most important of these are language and literacy competence. For that reason, most of the research evaluating bilingual education has focused on these developments. Children's academic success is deeply tied to their proficiency in the language of schooling in both the spoken and written forms [54]. Both literacy and academic outcomes from bilingual education will be discussed together here, but a more detailed examination of how bilingual children develop literacy is provided in Chapter 4, and some discussion of the brain regions involved in this development is offered in Chapter 6.

The type of education program is only one of the factors that shapes children's academic progress. An interesting test case for the importance of other environmental influences comes from the U.S. A large proportion of bilingual children in the U.S. are Hispanic, and many of them live in low SES families and have poor educational outcomes (see below). However, many Hispanic children are native speakers of English and do not participate in bilingual education programs. Nonetheless, the education outcomes for the children who speak English at home are similar to those for whom Spanish is their home language and are enrolled in bilingual education; both groups have high dropout rates and poor academic success. In other words, the educational outcomes for Hispanic children cannot be traced simply to English proficiency or enrolment in bilingual (or transitional) education [55]. More complex and multidimensional thinking is required to understand educational outcomes for various groups and the role that the education program contributes to those outcomes. The success of bilingual education depends on details about the program, the languages involved, and demographic profiles of the students. Therefore, it is helpful to examine some specific programs on their own.

Spanish-English bilingual education in the United States

Possibly the largest cluster of bilingual education programs are those dedicated to Spanish-English bilingual children in the U.S., so not surprisingly, this group has also been the focus of a large portion of the research. But as we saw, context matters, and the context in this case is very specific: In the United States, many people associate "bilingualism" with limited English proficiency and low socioeconomic status, both of which negatively impact school achievement [15]. Approximately 10% of all students in the United States are designated as English Language Learners, with the majority of them being Spanish-English bilinguals. Most of them are also low in socioeconomic status.

When the Bilingual Education Act was passed in the U.S. in 1968, there was little support for those programs, so the goals were redefined to make their purpose helping children develop English proficiency rather than making them bilingual. With this focus, English proficiency came at the expense of Spanish, the home language [56]. Spanish was used in school only as long as it was needed to establish English skills but then dropped as children were moved to English programs. However, research evaluating these programs revealed the benefits of building language skills in both languages. For example, Kathryn Lindholm-Leary and Nicholas Block [57] assessed the English and mathematics achievement of 659 Hispanic students whose first language was Spanish. The children were attending either mainstream English programs or various types of Spanish-English bilingual programs in California. Surprisingly, English proficiency scores were higher for students who were in the bilingual programs than for children who were in the English program, even though they only used English in school. A similar study by the same group followed 283 children from kindergarten through second grade [58]. All the children spoke both English and Spanish, but they entered kindergarten in either an English program or a bilingual program. At the beginning of kindergarten, children in the English programs had higher English scores than did those entering the bilingual programs, as one would expect. However, this difference disappeared within one or two years and then reversed. By the end of second grade, children in the bilingual program outperformed children in the English program in both English and Spanish test scores. There were other costs to being in the English program as well, because those children lost Spanish proficiency over these years, which, in fact, made them less bilingual. The loss of the home language proficiency is an outcome of these educational choices that is rarely discussed but has significant consequences for children's long-term development and socialization.

We know that academic and cognitive outcomes of Spanish-English bilingual children are poor when compared to non-Hispanic children [55], but there are several possible reasons for those outcomes. We designed a study to evaluate how children's level of bilingual proficiency might contribute to those results in these results [59]. We studied a group of children who shared many background features but differed in how bilingual they were. They were 8- to 11-year-old Spanish-English bilingual children in California living in challenging socioeconomic circumstances. We gave them cognitive tasks that have typically been performed better by bilingual children than by monolinguals (see Chapter 5). All the children performed more poorly than the middle-class children for whom we used the same tasks. However, the more bilingual the children were, in that their English and Spanish proficiency scores were more similar to each other, the better were their cognitive test scores. Even in a context where children are struggling in school, being more bilingual was associated with better cognitive performance.

Bilingual education in the world

Bilingual education programs serve a wide range of communities, comprise a broad selection of languages, and are situated in a range of countries. In some cases, students belong to the dominant culture and speak the community language, in other cases the children are part of minority groups and need to learn the community language, and in other cases they may enjoy socioeconomic advantages compared to monolingual children. For children in bilingual education programs, therefore, multiple factors determine academic success regardless of the educational program. Does the efficacy of bilingual education depend on these factors?

One well-studied example of a bilingual education program is Canadian French immersion in which Anglophone children who live in an English-speaking community are educated through French. The programs were created in the 1960s by monolingual Anglophone parents who wanted their children to learn French to a higher level than was taking place in schools. In the early years, many evaluation studies demonstrated that the programs were successful in maintaining English language proficiency and academic abilities while also instilling high levels of French proficiency, which reassured parents that this educational experiment did not have harmful consequences [60]. Subsequent research over the past 50 years has shown that English outcomes are equivalent to or better than those found for children in English programs, and French outcomes are moderate to high, although below levels found for native-speaking French children [61-63]. In terms of the original goals of developing French proficiency while maintaining high levels of academic achievement, the programs have been successful.

An interesting change is that the demographic profile of the children in these programs has evolved over the years. In the beginning, they were primarily monolingual English-speaking middle-class, but recently they are more diverse, including those who speak neither English nor French at home and have a broader range of socioeconomic backgrounds. The outcomes for these children in French Immersion has not been well-studied, but the issue is important for understanding what happens when they are educated in a language that is different from that of the home. Therefore, in addition to evaluating bilingual education, examining children in this program can also address the education of bilingual children. The few studies that have examined this question for French Immersion have produced mixed results [64, 65] but a recent one has been more clear. We followed 235 children in French Immersion between first grade and third grade as they learned French. We classified those who only knew English when they started the program as monolingual, and those who spoke a language other than English or French at home as bilingual. None of the children knew any French when they entered the program. However, by the end of the third year, the bilingual children who spoke a heritage language at home made significantly more progress in learning French than did children who were monolingual when they entered the program [66].

Other bilingual education programs aimed at middle class children have produced similar results. Three examples come from programs operating in Italian and English, Mandarin and English, and Hebrew and Russian. The Italian-English program took place in California, U.S.A. and was assessed in a small-scale study that included 60 children [67]. The researchers followed these children for three years, from first through third grades, and tested them each year for language and literacy ability in English and Italian. Beginning in first grade, the children demonstrated strong literacy skills in both Italian and English, even though instruction was exclusively in Italian, a pattern that continued through the course of the study.

The second program, also implemented in California, provided instruction through Mandarin beginning in kindergarten to children who either had Mandarin exposure at home or were only English speaking [68]. Like the Italian-English program, this was a small-scale study and, as well, all the children gained proficiency in both English and Mandarin and importantly achieved at least equivalent and sometimes greater than state levels on standardized tests of English, math and science in spite of being educated through Mandarin.

Finally, two studies investigated language and literacy development in Russian-Hebrew bilingual 4-year-olds who were attending either bilingual Hebrew-Russian or Hebrew schools in Israel, where Hebrew is the community language. Again, children in the bilingual programs developed language proficiency [69] and narrative skills [70] in Hebrew at least as well as did children in the Hebrew only programs, and at the same time maintained higher levels of Russian. Across all these studies, therefore, the language of the community was mastered whether or not it was the primary language of instruction. However, reaching high levels of proficiency in the home language that differed from the community language required educational support.

Unlike the studies of bilingual education in the U.S. with Hispanic children, these programs did not draw from low socioeconomic communities: children in the Italian-English program were described as "middle class"; children in the Mandarin-English program were described as "upper middle class"; and children in the Hebrew-Russian program were described as "mid-level socioeconomic". Even though none of the students was at-risk in the manner understood for Hispanic children in Spanish-English bilingual programs, the language and literacy outcomes were similar. Children progressed in both the language used for school instruction and the language of the community. Therefore, there is no evidence that education through two languages or through a language that is different from the community language impedes progress in the development of language and literacy skills in the majority language.

Other versions of bilingual education exist as well, including two-way immersion in which children with different home languages come together in school to learn each other's languages; heritage language programs to preserve the home language by including it in the school curriculum; and revitalization bilingual education in which threatened heritage languages used primarily by indigenous populations are introduced as the language of schooling to maintain it and preserve the culture. Evaluations of the success of each program must be carried out in the context of its specific intentions and expectations because these are always different. Moreover, these evaluations must be based on a sense of what educational outcomes would have been obtained if everything were constant except for the bilingual programming, a standard that is essentially impossible to meet. In other words, we would need to know how that individual child would have performed had she been enrolled in a different program. This is a bit like deciding whether the route you took was better or worse than the alternative if you had left at exactly the same time with exactly the same traffic conditions: you simply never know! For these reasons, our conclusions may reflect more "art" than "science". However, the results from these studies across all programs support two conclusions. First, there is no evidence that bilingual education impedes children's academic achievement. Second, if there are different outcomes from children in bilingual programs than those in standard monolingual programs, they tend to favor the bilingual programs. What is clear is that children in bilingual programs learn more language than children in monolingual programs. Not a bad return if there truly is no cost.

What if children have special needs?

The diversity of human ability is magnificently distributed through the population: some people are naturally gifted musicians and others cannot hear the difference between two notes; some people can create images in paint that elicit powerful emotional responses and others cannot copy a square with a ruler; some people can mentally perform abstract calculations based on hypothetical assumptions and others struggle to do basic arithmetic. Likewise, some children easily learn no matter what structure is provided, and others require carefully constructed support systems to establish basic skills. These children are sometimes given standardized tests to determine their learning abilities, and then sometimes they are diagnosed with a condition that interferes with learning. Should they be enrolled in bilingual education programs? Should they even become bilingual?

The issue of how to best educate children with special needs is of course not unique to bilingual education; it is an ongoing and pervasive problem for all education systems. However, the question is particularly acute for the former for two reasons. First, the most common challenge for children with learning difficulties is related to language impairment, a situation that may be made worse for those learning two languages. Second, the instruments and procedures by which these children are identified are based on test results from monolingual children and may not be sensitive to developmental progress in bilingual children. The two issues overlap to the extent that language disorders are identified by language tests developed for monolingual children.

Assessing bilingual children

Assessment is the foundation of any educational system and is also an enormous and highly profitable industry. Private companies, often affiliated with Publishing Houses, develop instruments for evaluating abilities. The scores from those tests allow educators to identify children whose scores fall outside the "normal" range. The reason the scores can be interpreted in order to make decisions about individual children's abilities is because all traits and abilities are assumed to be normally distributed through a population so that there are precise expectations for the likelihood of an individual having a particular value for that trait. This normal distribution is shown in Figure 3. The center point, indicated on Figure 3 as 0, is the average score for any test, trait, or ability for the entire population, and deviations from that center in both directions are symmetrical and orderly. The value associated with each boundary beyond 0 is determined by the standard deviation, or σ. The percentage figures indicated at the top of the graph show the proportion of the population expected to fall within each range. For example, the mean intelligence score (IQ) for the population is 100, and the standard deviation is 15, so the properties of the normal distribution mean that 68% of the population will have an IQ between 85 and 115 (see Chapter 5). This means that close to 70 out of 100 children fall in this middle range. Scores higher and lower than those in this central band become increasingly unlikely. If we include IQ scores between 70 and 130, we include 95% of the population. The remaining 5 out of 100 children have scores that fall outside that range. Determining where a child's score fits within a normal distribution, therefore, is a simple way to see how the child compares to the rest of the population. These calculations are used to decide if they would benefit from extra support (special education) or additional stimulation (gifted education). Too easy, right?

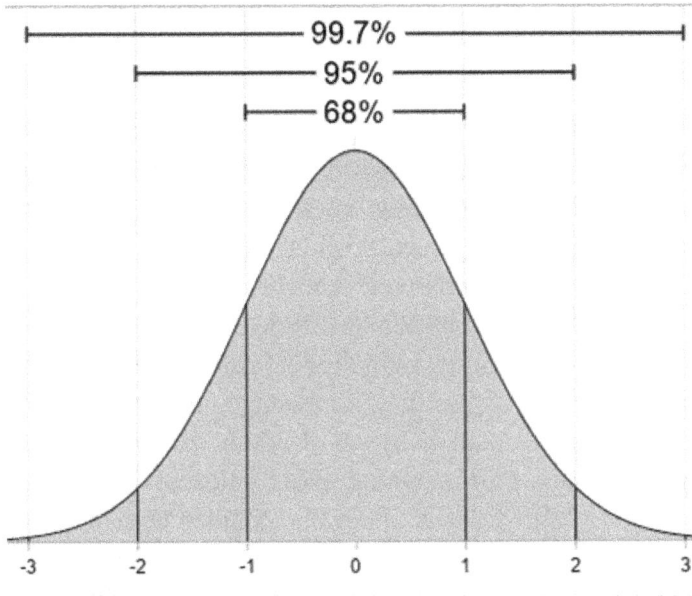

Figure 3. Normal distribution curve showing frequency for percent population by score.

Take children's vocabulary as an example. Vocabulary size is easily measured by standardized tests and, like all such tests, the results are represented by a normal distribution. Moreover, vocabulary size is a good predictor of verbal intelligence, and verbal intelligence is strongly related to overall intelligence. However, if we measure the vocabulary of monolingual children and compare it to bilingual children for that language, then monolingual children on average score higher than their bilingual counterparts. The latter, of course, also know another language, and their combined vocabulary across languages may well be higher than that of monolingual children in a single language, but vocabulary assessments do not provide that information.

One popular test of English vocabulary is the Peabody Picture Vocabulary test (PPVT) [71]. It is easy to administer, and the results have been standardized for populations ranging from 3- to over 80 years old, making it appropriate for the whole lifespan. However, those standardized scores were calculated from results obtained from populations that are essentially monolingual. The properties of the distribution for PPVT scores are the same as those for IQ tests,

namely, a mean of 100 and standard deviation of 15. Considering
only children, Figure 4 shows the PPVT test results for 1,738
children between the ages of 4 and 10 years [72]. The test score is
indicated on the horizontal axis, so points further to the right
represent higher vocabulary scores. The vertical axis is frequency, or
number of children obtaining each score, and in a normal
distribution the greatest frequency is in the middle range. As shown,
the results for both monolingual and bilingual children take the
shape of a normal distribution (as shown in Figure 3), but the
curves are shifted so that the monolingual curve is to the right of the
bilingual curve. This shows that, on average, monolingual children
obtain higher scores than bilingual children. However, there is a
substantial overlap of the two curves indicated by the double-
headed arrow. That designated region includes both monolingual
and bilingual children, so it is equally possible for bilingual children
to have a higher English vocabulary score than monolingual
children, despite the overall result showing higher average scores for
monolingual children. This example points to a problem of
interpreting test scores for bilingual children. It may simply be more
difficult or less reliable to use these distributions for clinical
assessment to identify children with special needs.

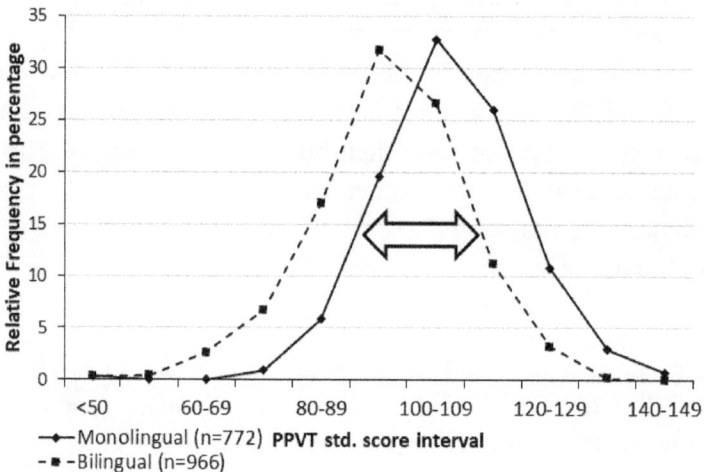

Figure 4. English vocabulary in monolingual and bilingual children.
Data from Bialystok et al. [72]

Language disorders, learning disorders, and bilingual children

Special Education programs are offered to children who require extra support to achieve grade expectations. Standardized tests are typically used to identify those who are eligible for these programs, a decision largely determined by their position on a normal distribution. But as we have seen, there are several reasons why they might occupy lower positions on these distributions and some of them have nothing to do with a learning disability. For verbal tests, for example, children from low socioeconomic contexts and bilingual children may score below their counterparts even in the absence of specific cognitive challenges. It is not surprising, therefore, that children from low socioeconomic families and bilingual children with poor English proficiency are overly represented in Special Education, at least in the United States [14]. Therefore, to evaluate the language, academic, and cognitive development of children with special needs, the most important decision is choosing the standard against which their abilities and progress will be measured. The first idea might be to compare bilingual children in Special Education programs or with diagnoses of learning impairment to bilingual children without such challenges. However, that comparison would undoubtedly indicate greater challenges for the children with special needs. Instead, the only meaningful comparison is between monolingual children and bilingual children who have been matched on all relevant variables, including the identification and degree of a language impairment. This is extremely difficult to do: language impairments may appear differently for monolingual and bilingual children, but it is the only way to determine if bilingualism interacts with these underlying conditions to produce special challenges for them. This is an important but unfortunately small area of ongoing research.

Another obstacle for identifying special needs for bilingual children is the range of terms and designations used to refer to a diffuse set of learning challenges. The original term for a language disorder that occurs in the absence of other cognitive problems was Specific Language Impairment (SLI) and was defined in terms a language disability in the absence of other cognitive impairments [73]. SLI is a neurodevelopmental disorder that is estimated to affect approximately 7% of the general population. Because it disrupts neurocognitive development, it leads to difficulties in language learning that appear as delayed language development. However, the criteria for this diagnosis have become fuzzy, largely because it was rare to find there was in fact no associated cognitive challenges. More recent research has used different terminology and somewhat modified descriptions for what is essentially this same condition, including Developmental Language Disorder (DLD), Primary Language Impairment (PLI), and Specific Learning Disability (SLD).

These language disorders are difficult to diagnose but they are especially problematic for bilingual children. Some of the salient markers for these disorders are part of normal language development for bilingual children. Children with a clinical language disorder and bilingual children may both experience delayed language acquisition or smaller vocabulary levels than generally expected. How can one determine, therefore, if a child has a clinical language delay or is a typically developing child learning two languages? In a series of studies addressing this question, Kathryn Kohnert and colleagues [74] concluded that bilingual children perform similarly to monolingual children with language impairment on many language tasks but consistently perform similarly to typically-developing monolingual children on cognitive tasks. In other words, only language proficiency scores do not line up with other typically developing children. Recall this was the original definition of Specific Language Impairment, but that definition was revised when it was found that those children in fact did have a variety of other cognitive impairments. Bilingual children with delayed language acquisition, in contrast, may simply be taking longer to learn language. The important caution, therefore, is to refrain from overinterpreting language delays in bilingual children in terms of clinical impairments.

The body of literature that carefully investigates the interplay between bilingualism and language disorders is relatively small, so most of the conclusions are tentative. In an extensive survey of this research, Johanne Paradis [75] reviewed studies comparing bilingual children to monolingual children, both with Specific Language Impairment, and bilingual children with SLI to bilingual children experiencing typical development. These contrasts pointed to unique features of bilingual language development that were different from that of monolingual children. Her conclusion was that there was no evidence that bilingualism added to the challenges presented by SLI; there is no double handicap to language learning that comes from being bilingual for children with SLI.

Finally, as described above, a significant barrier to assessment is that the instruments were standardized for monolingual children, and in most cases, monolingual speakers of English. In the United States, most of the assessment of bilingual children and discussion about bilingual education is related to Spanish-English bilingualism. Because both languages can be identified and assessed, it opens the possibility of testing children in both of them, something that is not possible if the second language is one of many different languages for which testing instruments are not available. Having information of children's abilities in both languages substantially increases the reliability of detecting and diagnosing language impairments. These bilingual instruments are now being constructed and tested, with promising results [76-78]. This is an important initiative that will provide the tools for more accurate assessments in the future, and the possibility of serving a larger community.

Is bilingual education for everyone?

There is no single meaning of the term "bilingual education." Children are educated in multiple languages, or in a language different from the primary one used at home for many reasons, including as a means of learning a foreign language to a high level of proficiency, maintaining a heritage language that is not used in the community, integrating into a culture to learn the community language that is different from the home language, among others. Moreover, these situations carry different degrees of choice; learning the language of the community, for example, is probably a more pressing need than is learning a foreign language. For that reason, pressure on parents to decide to enroll their children in these programs is motivated by different factors, and the consequences of the decision vary widely. So, the question about the universal appropriateness of bilingual education for all children depends on the type of program under consideration, and only then can the unique needs and profile of individual children be considered.

Overall, studies evaluating a range of bilingual education programs have produced positive results. These studies assess language achievement, academic achievement, or basic cognitive development. In some cases, the results are considered positive because there is no difference in outcome in at least some domains between children in the bilingual program and comparable children in a standard program, showing that the bilingual program has not compromised learning. In other cases, children in bilingual programs achieve more than their peers in standard programs, most often in the language domain, but sometimes in academic and cognitive assessments as well, which makes the program beneficial for learning. Although there are essentially no studies that show better outcomes for standard programs than for bilingual ones, this may happen for individual children. So, what are parents to do?

Children who have clinical learning impairments, particularly language impairments, will find an educational program based on intense language demands to be challenging. However, the relevant question is the extent to which they would find the program *more* challenging than they would a standard program. Further, what is the balance between whatever challenges are brought by a bilingual program and its possible benefits? These are theoretical questions to the extent they apply to groups of children and personal questions to the extent they apply to an individual child. Because of these competing tensions, there are no absolute answers, but the research can provide some guidance. The general pattern of research results with bilingual children with language impairment is that they are not additionally burdened by these programs [75], but that outcome might not be good enough for parents who want their children's education to be as stress-free as possible, perhaps leaving time in their children's lives to devote to directly addressing their learning needs. At the same time, the opportunity to learn another language must be considered as well. As Kathryn Kohnert [79] argues, if you take away one language from a bilingual child with a learning disability, you are left with a monolingual child with a learning disability! Ultimately, however, educational choices are complex and personal.

Individual stories are always a good source for counterevidence. Some years ago, the headmaster of an elite International School that offered a bilingual program told me that there was resistance from some of the families towards the bilingual program. He explained that some of the students were attending the school because their families were there only temporarily, often for one or two years, and then would be returning to their home country. Therefore, these children were *also* completing the curriculum of their home country after school every day, which of course was offered in a language different from either of the languages in the bilingual school program. The parents requested that their child be exempt from the bilingual portion of the curriculum: it was too much work and the poor grades in that language would compromise their record, possibly impacting their entry to a good university in their home country. Perhaps the parents were right, but the headmaster declined.

Another story is about an eminent colleague who is fluent in many languages. However, he spent his childhood in a country different from the one where he was born, and the language of his education as well as his language of childhood socializing was different from his home language, the one he still considers to be his native language. He told me that, at least as a child, he felt that there was no language in which he was perfectly fluent or completely comfortable. But of course, this is a person with *very* high standards!

There may be special circumstances or individual factors that rule against bilingual education for some children. However, the point about educational alternatives is that they are options, and the more choice one has, the better decisions can be made. Bilingual education may not be the best fit for everyone, but the available research across the spectrum of such programs is that they come with no additional risk to children's development, at least for most of them. It's just good to have a choice.

Take-away conclusions

- Difference between *bilingual education* (educational programs conducted in two languages) and the *education of bilingual children* (the experience of bilingual children in school)
- Bilingual education programs are different in many ways, but produce good educational outcomes overall
- Selecting the best program for bilingual children with special learning needs requires an overall assessment of the motivations and challenges associated with each possible choice

Chapter 4
Learning to Read

Every parent knows the thrill of driving through town, thinking of nothing in particular, young child buckled firmly in the back seat, when a high-pitched voice from behind says: "What's a Foot Locker"? The child can read! Becoming literate is a significant milestone in children's development. It gives them access to levels of understanding of the world around them, and an independence in navigating it that is not available to children who cannot read. There is a magical moment when kids have figured out literacy and cannot refrain from reading everything they see: street signs, cereal boxes, random papers carelessly left around the house. Suddenly the world is awash in meaning!

Nevertheless, reading is not an inevitable outcome of learning language. Many developments and insights are needed to be in place for children to become independent readers. Obviously, they need to have a strong basis of language knowledge, including adequate vocabulary and knowledge about structure: what we might call "grammar". They also need to understand the units of speech that make up the language they hear and be able to recognize the individual sounds and syllables. Beyond those units, they must be aware of the structure of stories that produce meaningful discourse. And finally, maybe most importantly, they must possess the cognitive resources to translate printed symbols into the familiar sounds of spoken language using whatever translation process is required by the writing system used in that language. These abilities develop over several years and are greatly enhanced through experience; by far, the most important intervention for helping children to become literate is reading stories to them, lots of stories and in all the languages they know! But if children are being raised with two languages, is their progress in acquiring literacy affected? Does learning to read in one language guarantee literacy in the other? Or does the need to learn to read in two languages simply become overwhelming?

Unlike the acquisition of spoken language, there are enormous individual differences in children's progress in learning to read. Some learn to read in school following a structured curriculum that moves them through the stages; others struggle despite excellent teaching and tutoring; and some of them appear to read spontaneously and effortlessly, even before reading is introduced in school. The range of abilities that children bring to the task and the variety of outcomes found as they cautiously enter the world of the literate have been the topics of much research. Although clear conclusions are still some distance off, the research has succeeded in describing the essential components of the variability in acquiring literacy (for an overview of this research, see the work of Peter Afflerbach [80]).

But what about children who speak more than one language and are learning to read in one or both of them? The question may appear simple, but the answers are complex and depend on a host of specific situations. For example: (a) does the child already speak two languages and is therefore adding literacy to a known spoken language?, (b) is the child learning a second language and the literacy associated with that language at the same time, a situation that generally takes place in school?, (c) is that school language also used in the home?, and (d) is the child learning to read in two languages written in the same or different writing systems or scripts? Each of these issues creates different challenges for children learning to read.

Languages are written in different ways, but to understand what those differences are, we first need a brief look at how linguists divide up language. The smallest unit of speech is a *phoneme*: the word DOG has three phonemes; the word DOGGY has 4 phonemes. The set of phonemes that can be uttered together is a *syllable*: the word DOG has one syllable; the word DOGGY has two syllables. The smallest unit that has meaning is a *morpheme*: the word DOG has one morpheme (small animal); the word DOGS has two morphemes (small animal plus plural). All these units —

phoneme, syllable, and morpheme — can be the basis for translating speech to print.

Languages are written in one of three main writing systems and each of them is based on a different one of these units. In alphabetic systems, symbols represent individual sounds, or phonemes (e.g., English; A, B). In a syllabic system or syllabary, the symbols represent the sounds in a whole syllable (e.g., several Indigenous languages such as Ojibwe; ᐅ, ᐋ). In morphophonetic writing systems, symbols represent both units of meaning through morphemes and include phonemic information (e.g., Chinese; 正體字). And just to keep it very confusing, Japanese uses both syllabic and morphophonetic systems, and Korean combines elements of alphabetic and syllabic writing. Syllabaries might be the most intuitive writing system and were used in very early writing systems, such as Linear B, although there were alphabetic writing systems before then, notably Phoenician. However, syllabaries were the choice of European missionaries to the New World who created writing systems for the oral Indigenous languages they encountered in North America (Central and South American Indigenous communities had their own writing systems). Within each writing system, the set of symbols that are used also varies: English is written in Roman script (A, B) and Russian is written in Cyrillic script (А, Б), although both are alphabetic writing systems. Similarly, Mandarin is written in simplified characters and Cantonese is written in traditional characters although both are morphophonetic writing systems. Therefore, script becomes another potential difference even within the same writing system.

All of these factors matter, and all of them have an impact on how children progress in learning to read. The different relations between languages and the systems in which they are written affect children's success in learning to read in more than one language. There is no single answer to the question about the effect of bilingualism on learning to read and becoming biliterate.

The reading wars

How strange to use military language to describe pedagogical controversies, but that is exactly what has happened in the debate about reading instruction. The disagreement that led to "the war" is based on a dichotomy which, like all dichotomies, is overly simplistic: Which is the "proper" approach to reading? Instruction through the sound-symbol correspondences that connect the units of print to spoken language (phonics), or instruction through the wholistic recognition of words that convey meaning (whole word)? The phonics-whole word debate was fierce through the 1980s [81] and has not disappeared [82]. Note, however, that there is a hint of language nationalism in the debate: the question only applies to alphabetic languages, the writing system that is primarily the domain of the powerful west. The reading wars were largely waged around how to teach children to read English.

Within the context of the sound (phonics) versus meaning (whole word) debate, several models of reading have been proposed to explain how children learn to read. Some of them explicitly side with one or the other reading army, and others try to propose a treaty that incorporates elements of each. One such popular model is called the Simple View of Reading [83] and, as the name suggests, it is indeed simple. The assumption is that the primary goal of reading is comprehension. To that end, reading comprehension is explained by the combination of decoding ability (interpreting the marks on the page) and language comprehension (understanding what the text means). To some extent, therefore, the Simple View of Reading sidesteps the reading wars by including elements of both phonics and meaning. To the extent that children learn how to translate the symbols into sounds and integrate them into meaningful sentences, they will read.

Despite the neat solution, the Simple View of Reading becomes problematic when applied to bilingual children. In early research, this model was investigated in studies of Spanish-English bilingual children learning to read in the United States and was declared to be a successful fit. However, that is a very particular demographic. For learning to read in two languages, decoding ability depends on the writing systems used in each language and the relations between them. Both Spanish and English use an alphabetic system, which should make learning to read in both easy, but the decoding rules are different. Spanish has very reliable sound-symbol relations in which letters always have the same sound; English, in contrast, has notoriously unreliable sound-symbol correspondences (-INT, as in "pint" or "hint"; -OUGH, as in "bough" or "through"). Children need to have different expectations when decoding print in Spanish or in English, even though both contain the same letters. The Simple View of Reading also places importance on language proficiency which is largely determined by vocabulary. Children rarely, if ever, have equal proficiency in both languages, and in the case of Spanish-English bilingual children, there may be other challenges to developing adequate proficiency to support reading. As we saw in Chapter 1, Spanish-English bilingual children in the U.S. are often from low socioeconomic backgrounds, and those contexts are associated with poorer language development and smaller vocabulary. So, what should we expect when these children are learning to read? The Simple View of Reading has largely been able to explain literacy development in Spanish-English bilingual children [84], at least by pointing to the elements of reading that must be mastered for both languages. For example, decoding is easier in Spanish than in English but comprehension depends on vocabulary in each language. The application of this model to learning to read in other languages, however, is less certain.

The reading wars have dominated the discussion of literacy instruction for decades, but they are based almost entirely on teaching literacy in alphabetic languages, and more to the point, English. The debate takes on new complexities when children are learning to read in two languages that may not share a writing system or script. In those cases, whatever mechanism is involved in understanding reading may rest on different basic knowledge. Many of those complexities are yet to be discovered.

How much language?

It is obvious that learning to read requires knowing language, and much research has documented the important role of oral language proficiency on reading development. Knowledge of language, here defined in terms of vocabulary size, is one of the two factors in the Simple View of Reading. It is also well-known that the single most important factor that influences vocabulary size is socioeconomic status (SES): children in lower SES environments know fewer words than children in more affluent families, as described in Chapter 1 [21]. These children are also more likely than higher SES children to struggle in school and encounter challenges when learning to read. This initial language delay continues to play out through the school years as children from low SES environments on average fall further behind.

Like low SES children compared to high SES children, bilingual children know fewer words in each language when compared to monolingual children who speak only one of those languages. Although some researchers argue that the gap is erased if vocabulary is measured in both languages [85], others claim there is still a difference between monolingual and bilingual children [86]. This point was illustrated in Chapter 3. But does this vocabulary limitation impose a burden similar to that experienced by low SES children when learning to read? The short answer is no, it does not.

If vocabulary is measured in only one language, typically the language of schooling, then children who speak something different at home have had less exposure to that language and, like the low SES children described above, have had less opportunity to build that vocabulary. Children are learning different words at home and at school, and vocabulary tests typically include both, but the words that are most important for academic success are the school words.

My colleagues and I had the opportunity to demonstrate this point in the study of English receptive vocabulary described in Chapter 3 [72]. Although the results for all children were well described by a normal bell curve (see Figure 4) and the average scores were all close to the overall average of 100, the average score for children who additionally spoke a non-English language at home was significantly lower than was the score for the monolingual children, approximately 95 vs. approximately 105. Similar results were found in a study of 1,605 adults [87]. Yet these average scores ignore the fact that bilinguals also know words in at least one other language. In many cases, the words they know in both languages refer to different concepts, so there is no sense in which their vocabulary score in only one language can be interpreted as a "deficit." Therefore, we need more information about how the overall vocabulary of bilingual children breaks down.

We examined vocabulary in more detail in a subset of 161 6-year-olds from the large study described above. All the children in that study were living in an English-speaking community and attending schools in which all instruction was conducted in English. The non-English languages of the bilingual children included dozens of different languages, and so it would have been impossible to give children vocabulary tests in all of them. Our approach instead was to look more carefully at the English words to see if there was any pattern in the types of words that were known by monolingual and bilingual children. We divided the words into two categories indicating the likelihood that they were learned and used in the home environment or the school environment. Thus, words referring to food, family, and home activities were considered "home" words, including such items as "squash", "camcorder" (the study was done a long time ago!), "pitcher". In contrast, words referring to abstractions, professions, school activities were considered "school" words, including such items as "astronaut", "raccoon", "rectangle". For monolingual children, there was no difference between their scores on home words and school words. That was not the case for bilingual children. For this group, English vocabulary scores were higher for school words than home words, but more importantly, their scores on school words were equivalent to those of the monolingual children. Put another way, all of the English vocabulary difference between groups could be explained by knowledge of "home" words. Scores for the English words that came from their classroom experience were the same for all the children, and these presumably are the words most important for literacy and other forms of academic achievement. Essentially, the results show that bilingual children are more likely to name foods and family activities in the non-English language. In short, there is no evidence for anything that approaches a "vocabulary deficit" for bilingual children once the full range of their linguistic knowledge is considered.

Whether or not there are differences in vocabulary level between monolingual and bilingual children, does children's level of language proficiency impact learning to read? In the Simple View of Reading, decoding and comprehension are partly determined by children's language proficiency. What happens if bilingual children begin with lower levels of language proficiency?

One study that examined this question tested 60 bilingual children to see if there was a relation between vocabulary size and reading ability [88]. About 60% of the children spoke English and Spanish, and about 40% spoke English and an Asian language, the majority being Chinese. Notably, however, there was also a difference in socioeconomic status between these two non-English language groups because the Asian families had higher education than the Hispanic families. Parents' education is important for children's literacy development, so this difference is not trivial. There was a significant relation between children's English vocabulary and both decoding and comprehension measures on English reading tests for both language groups. This is the prediction from the Simple View of Reading, so the authors concluded that the model applies well to bilingual children learning to read regardless of SES or the other language.

These results endorse a model of reading that is widely used in studies of literacy acquisition in monolinguals that puts most of the importance on language proficiency. By confirming a connection between English vocabulary, which is the second language for these children, and English reading achievement, the results set out clear pedagogical implications: improve language proficiency for bilingual children and reading will follow. But how guaranteed is that outcome? The study leaves several questions unanswered. There were no monolingual children, so we do not know how their literacy development would compare to that of monolingual children. More striking, however, is that there is little information on how this simple relation between vocabulary and reading works for children learning to read in two languages that are written in different ways. No comparisons were reported between the Spanish and Asian subgroups, so no conclusions can be made about potential differences in those relations. Moreover, no information was provided about whether these children were also learning to read in their other language. Would decoding be easier for Spanish-English bilinguals for whom the two writing systems were comparable, or more difficult for Asian-English bilinguals for whom one of the languages may not even use an alphabetic system?

We investigated this question in an early study with children in first grade just learning to read. They belonged to one of four groups: English monolingual children, Spanish-English bilingual children (same writing systems, same scripts), Hebrew-English bilingual children (same writing systems, different scripts), and Chinese-English bilingual children (different writing systems) [89]. All the children were tested for their ability to decode new words, their understanding of the units of language (sound, word, meaning), and vocabulary size. The children in the three bilingual groups completed these tests in both languages. The results were different for the four groups. Children whose non-English language was written alphabetically (Spanish, Hebrew) had better awareness of the units of sound than the Chinese bilingual group whose other language is not written alphabetically. Moreover, the reading scores in the two languages were correlated for children whose two languages were written in the same writing system, that is, alphabetically, but unrelated for the Chinese-English bilinguals whose languages used different writing systems. Children appear to extrapolate what they know about reading in one language and apply it to reading in the other language, but this only works if the two languages are written in the same system.

To summarize, the research largely supports the view that the models used to explain literacy development in monolingual children apply as well to bilingual children. This is a good thing because it means that the approaches used in literacy pedagogy are appropriate for bilingual children.

Ellen Bialystok

Language as an object: metalinguistic awareness

The main difference between spoken language and written language is the invisibility of the former and the objective reality of the latter. Children learn to speak without any idea that words are made up of sounds and need to be combined according to rules of grammar; they only care that the words they choose and the order in which they utter them will get them what they want. Things work differently for written language. Since all written language is a transcription of spoken language, the units that are transcribed into print must be clear. For alphabetic languages, these are sounds; for character languages, these are morphemes. The knowledge of these written units and awareness of their existence as separate from their meanings is called "metalinguistic awareness". It is the understanding that language has an objective structure and is one of the foundations for acquiring literacy.

Some of the earliest research with bilingual children compared their development to that of similar monolingual children as they acquired metalinguistic awareness [90]. If there is a developmental difference between monolingual and bilingual children, it seems reasonable that it is most likely to emerge in concepts about language. The understanding of the formal properties of language as distinct from their meanings is essential to all high-level uses of languages, and certainly to the development of literacy. How do children come to realize that the word "dog" contains three sounds, that the word "snow" is not cold, or that the word "caterpillar" is bigger than the word "whale", even though it refers to a smaller thing? These are all aspects of metalinguistic awareness, and they are all essential for literacy.

Research conducted during the 1970s and 1980s confirmed predictions that bilingual children had better metalinguistic awareness than monolingual children. One type of study consisted in giving them grammar tests in which they had to decide if sentences were grammatically correct or not, or as it was explained to children, said the "right way" or the "wrong way". The grammatical error could be placed in any structure that the researchers were investigating. In some cases, children were also asked to explain why the sentence was not said the right way and, possibly, correct it in order to demonstrate some explicit knowledge of the rule. The typical finding was that bilingual children performed these tasks better than monolingual children, and these results were used to conclude that knowledge of two languages facilitates children's understanding of the underlying structure of any language [91]. If metalinguistic awareness develops earlier in bilingual children than in monolingual children, it should follow that the development of literacy will also develop earlier.

As research accumulated, however, the results seemed to be less consistent; some of these grammar judgement tasks were solved similarly by monolingual and bilingual children. In a series of studies we set out to find what features led to bilinguals performing these tasks better than monolingual children [92]. To do this, we adapted the standard judgement task to create four kinds of sentences. The first type of sentences, *correct*, were grammatically correct and meaningful ("Apples grow on trees") and the second type, *incorrect*, had a grammatical error ("Apples trees on grow"). These are the two types of sentences that had been used in most of those previous studies and provide information about children's knowledge of grammar. We then added two further sentence types. The third type, *anomalous*, were grammatically correct but silly ("Apples grow on noses"), and the fourth type, *wrong*, were incorrect for both grammar and meaning ("Apples noses on grow").

The instructions were always the same: Children were told to decide if the sentence was said the right way or the wrong way but to ignore the meaning. The important condition is the anomalous sentences because children had to pay attention to how they were formed, the grammar, and not get distracted by the silly meaning. But meaning is how we use and evaluate language, so instructions to ignore meaning are, by definition, unnatural. Across these studies, monolingual and bilingual children were equally able to determine if meaningful sentences were said the right way or the wrong way, but bilingual children were consistently more successful than monolingual children on the anomalous sentences. Bilingual children were able to look past the meaning and recognize that

"Apples grow on noses" is said the right way, however ridiculous the image. We concluded that there were indeed differences between monolingual and bilingual children in their ability to demonstrate metalinguistic awareness, but that those differences were not found in simple tests of language structure. It was only when additional demands were placed on the task, in this case, the need to ignore meaning, that differences between the language groups emerged.

In another example, we tested the metalinguistic notion that the meaning of the printed word comes entirely from the way it is written, not from what happens to be close to it [93]. When we read picture books to children, they see both print and images and we assume that they understand the story comes from the print, but that might not be the case. To demonstrate this idea, we showed two pictures to 3 and 4-years-old children. All of them could name and recognize printed letters, but none could read. Then we placed a card with the name of one of the pictures underneath, as shown in Figure 5.

We told the child what the card said, in this case, "dog" and asked the child to repeat it. Then there was an "accident" in which a stuffed animal raced across the table and the card got pushed over so it was under the other picture. After scolding the naughty stuffed animal, we again asked the child what the card said. This time, most of the monolingual children changed their answer to "tree". The bilingual children, in contrast, understand that the card still said "dog".

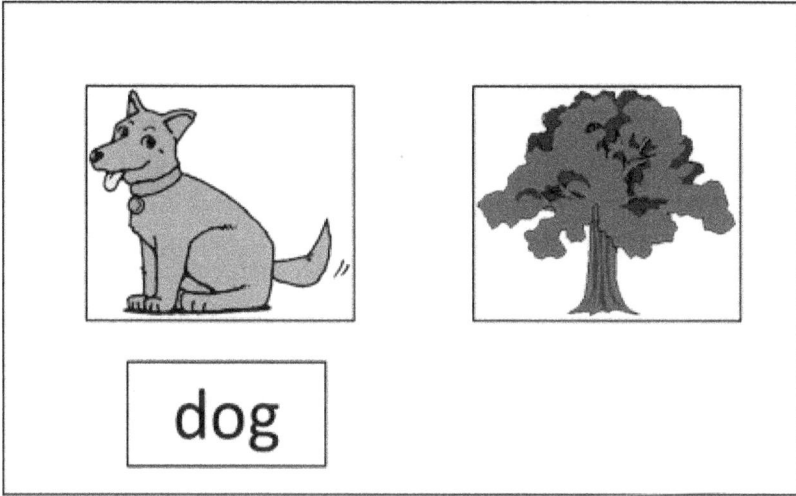

*Figure 5. Task in which children are asked what the word says
after it is "accidently" moved to be under the other picture.*

Both for judging the grammar of a silly sentence and for knowing that the word on the card did not change just because it moved, children need to attend to the information that is important (the grammar of the sentence or the letters in the word) and ignore what is irrelevant (the meaning of the sentence or the name of the other picture) even though these things are competing for the child's attention. In both these cases, children are asked to ignore linguistic information, but the ability to ignore a salient cue and not be distracted by it in order to come to the correct answer is a cognitive ability, even when it is applied to language. Therefore, the most important difference between monolingual and bilingual children was not simply in their ability to perform metalinguistic awareness tasks, but rather in the cognitive processes needed to perform them. These processes are discussed in Chapter 5.

The cognitive connection

If metalinguistic awareness has an important role in learning to read, and bilingual children perform metalinguistic tasks better than monolingual children, do they also enjoy an advantage in acquiring literacy? Literacy also requires language proficiency, and recall that bilingual children typically have a smaller vocabulary in each language than their monolingual counterparts. As we saw, however, the superior performance of bilingual children on metalinguistic tasks might be better understood in terms of cognitive processes rather than in notions of metalinguistic awareness. Therefore, understanding literacy acquisition needs an account of some of the cognitive underpinnings of reading and how they might differ for children who are learning to read in more than one language.

Unlike speaking, which seems to proceed effortlessly, reading engages a network of cognitive processes to recognize, interpret, and integrate the printed symbols to create meaning. Many of these cognitive processes, such as working memory that enables children to hold information in mind and manipulate it, have been investigated and shown to be central to reading, but the assumption is that the children in those studies were likely monolingual [94]. Yet, some research has extended these studies to bilingual children and found similar results [95]. Specifically, children with better working memory are more able to hold in mind relevant concepts and integrate text in real time than children with less capacity in this regard. This skill contributes to their success in reading. Several studies have demonstrated better working memory ability in bilingual children than in monolinguals [96].

Other cognitive abilities that support literacy are less obviously related to reading. For example, reading requires being able to take a perspective different from one's own. This ability may come more easily to bilingual children because they already understand that a thing can have two different names and that different people say the same thing in different ways. In perspective-taking tasks, children must anticipate what a complex visual display would look like from a different point of view: how does the doll I'm looking at appear to you when you are standing on the opposite side? Some studies have shown that bilingual children are better at these tasks than their monolingual peers [97]. Extending this notion to language, Hsin and Snow [98] compared the quality of essays of monolingual and bilingual children who were in fourth to sixth grades. Typically, bilingual children find writing tasks to be more difficult than oral tasks, presumably because of the greater need for vocabulary.

Nonetheless, the bilingual children in this study produced higher quality essays than the monolinguals in terms of the incorporation of a different perspective on an issue.

Finally, if there are substantial differences between the cognitive processes used by monolingual and bilingual children in learning to read, can these differences be found in the brain? In other words, are brain networks used differently by children in these language groups, and do the specific demands of each language modify those networks? Some research on this possibility is discussed in Chapter 6.

Learning to read

Learning to read sits on several foundations, including oral language proficiency, metalinguistic awareness, and cognitive processes used to engage in all complex tasks. There are no simple recipes to predict literacy acquisition by bilingual children, although all these ingredients must be included. In addition to variations in the foundational developments, one must consider the variety of situations described earlier: bilingual children may be learning to read in one or both of their languages, and those languages may share, or not, formal properties of how they are written, and therefore, require children to have knowledge about how writing works in that language. These foundations have an impact on the acquisition of literacy for bilingual children in different ways. Lower language proficiency and vocabulary possibly increase the challenge, but better metalinguistic awareness —possibly because it is a better skill in the underlying cognitive processes required for these tasks— facilitates literacy acquisition.

Three points are clear. First, there is no evidence that bilingualism itself is a deterrent to acquiring literacy in any of the child's languages, although there may be some difference in the timetable for achieving fluent reading. Second, drawing children's attention to the metalinguistic units that are the basis of the writing system provides them the tools to approach the written text. For alphabetic languages, these are phonemes, and children who are encouraged to examine the sounds of language by playing word games learn these concepts more quickly than those who do not. Conversations about rhyming and alliteration heighten children's sense of the phonemic structure of language. For character languages, the approach is less clear because each character conveys both phonological and semantic information, but possibly, familiarity with the visual forms prior to learning what they represent would be a useful background to learning to read. Finally, the most powerful avenue to learning to read is reading. Experience with stories improves every aspect of the linguistic and cognitive skills that are ultimately responsible for literacy. Through stories children learn new vocabulary and grammatical structure while they are engaged in figuring out meaning. And that, above all, is the purpose of literacy. So, to return to the simple suggestion made at the beginning of this chapter, just read!

Take-away conclusions

- Learning to read depends on adequate vocabulary, but even though bilingual children often have smaller vocabularies than monolingual children, there is no additional challenge to reading

- The progress bilingual children make in learning to read in their two languages depends on the relation between the way they are written

- Several of the cognitive abilities needed for literacy are better developed in bilingual children than in monolinguals, which potentially provides some advantage in learning to read

Chapter 5
Are Bilingual Children Smarter?

Do children who speak more than one language develop different cognitive abilities than children who speak only one? And if so, is that different path better for bilingual children? Does it make them somehow smarter? Or is it worse for these multilingual children, making them confused? The question taps into our basic need for simple answers: Is this good for my child or bad for my child? Between about 1920 and 1960, a large body of research explored this question and proclaimed that bilingualism was "bad".

But why should multilingualism change children's cognitive ability in either direction? The deceptively simple question about whether bilingualism is good or bad for children rests on a set of assumptions that have a long history of controversy in academic circles, namely, the relation between language and thought. According to many theorists, language and thought are different domains, occupy separate spheres, and undergo their own developmental trajectories. Therefore, for a language experience (bilingualism) to influence intellectual outcomes (thought), the two must be able to interact and influence each other. But this prerequisite has not always been met.

Until around 1960, psychology in North America was dominated by American psychologist B.F. Skinner's theory of behaviorism. In this view, there was no concept of "mind" because the belief was that we could only be sure of what we actually see, and since we cannot see "minds", or "thoughts", such notions were not acceptable objects of study for psychology. If psychology were to be accepted as a "science", it would have to stick to the "facts"! Psychology in Europe took a different path, but that is a separate story. In North America, psychology was limited to studying observable behavior. The basis of behaviorism was that all actions, including knowledge, are shaped by external reinforcement schedules that make it more or less likely that the action will be repeated. If an action, such as uttering a word, was followed by a positive outcome, such as an excited smile from mommy, that action became more likely to be repeated. This simple idea is still useful for some purposes: we provide positive reinforcement to children hoping that the good behavior they just showed will be repeated.

But increasing the likelihood that an action will be repeated is not the same as having a representation of that action in mind, or as we might say "knowing" something. Therefore, for behaviorism there was nothing in the "mind" corresponding to what we would call "thought", only actions that were repeated if they were reinforced. And without representations of knowledge in the mind, there was no way to consider their possible interaction with language experiences. This situation changed with the beginning of the "Cognitive Revolution" in the late 1950s that transformed the way psychologists thought about the mind. In this new approach to psychology, the full richness of the mind was acknowledged and explored, including memories, beliefs, desires, and processes such as attention, shifting, and control that allowed us to access and manipulate them [99]. However, it took about two decades for this new cognitive view to become the predominant paradigm in psychology and turn attention away from stimulus-response associations to the world of thinking, reasoning, and learning. The important part of the timeline is that during the period in which bilingualism was considered to be harmful to children, from around 1920 to 1960, there really was no concept of cognition or cognitive ability. That research on the impact of bilingualism, as we will see, used a proxy for cognition that was fraught with its own difficulties.

Linguistics remained an isolationist discipline for much longer than other fields of human cognition. During the time that Skinnerian behaviorism ruled psychology, linguistics was dominated by structuralist theories influenced by such theorists as the Swiss linguist Ferdinand de Saussure. The central notion was that languages were formal systems so their "properties and relations could be described." Crucially, however, language was not considered to be a feature of mind. Around 1960, at the same time as the cognitive revolution was getting underway, Noam Chomsky proposed generative grammar as a new theory of linguistics. The central idea was that language ability exists as a unique mental module [100]. Humans, on this view, are born with innate knowledge of linguistic structure, called universal grammar, and the processes required to expand this basic structure into native speaker competence of any natural language are put into play simply by exposure to a language community. In this way, language was finally placed inside the mind, but it was confined to a contained module and had little possibility of connecting with other forms of thought.

Therefore, until around 1960, the prevailing view was that language and thought were separate entities and both were externally determined with no foundation in the mind. With this architecture, there was no reasonable way to see how one could influence the other. However, a different formulation of the question regarding the potential impact of bilingualism did receive a great deal of attention. That early research was not concerned directly with cognition as such, but rather used an observable substitute for cognition. The research investigated "intelligence", and that is quite a different matter.

Intelligence and cognitive ability are often used interchangeably but they are fundamentally different. Intelligence refers to a feature of mind that is presumed to be constant over time; intelligence tests assess the efficiency or acuity of that mind. Cognitive ability refers to skill in carrying out specific mental functions; cognitive tests assess performance on those skills or processes. Put another way, intelligence describes a sort of capacity of the system and cognition describes how individuals can use that capacity to achieve goals. Intelligence levels are largely consistent across the lifespan but cognitive ability changes with experience, expertise, and development. The two are of course related; to the extent that intelligence is a general ability to acquire knowledge and skills, it is associated with positive outcomes in cognition. Both intelligence and cognition are influenced by a combination of genetic and experiential factors, although neither is wholly innate nor completely learned. The difference between intelligence and cognition and how we measure each of them is crucial to understanding what the original research meant for the development of bilingual children.

The intelligence argument

In the first half of the 20th century, a surprisingly large number of studies were published comparing the performance of monolingual and bilingual children on intelligence tests, and all concluded that there was "inferiority" for bilinguals. Some of the more influential studies described the "mental confusion" [20], "mental retardation" [101], and "language handicap" [102] that followed from bilingualism. These results were widely publicized and formed the basis for pervasive negative attitudes about bilingualism, some of which persist to this day. It is still the case that educators, clinicians, physicians, and other professionals sometimes advise the families of children who are struggling in school or appear to be delayed in developing language to remove one of the languages from the home, a recommendation for which there is no scientific support [79].   However, even during the time when these bleak outcomes from intelligence tests were widely reported and accepted, two major reviews of the research adopted a more moderate position. Natalie Darcy was a professor of Education who became interested in the question of bilingualism and intelligence. She conducted her own research and two major reviews of the existing literature [103, 104]. Her conclusion was that in well-controlled studies, monolingual children outperformed bilingual children on verbal intelligence tests, just as the majority of the research had shown. These tests evaluated such things as vocabulary, memory for words, manipulation of words and meanings, and so on (see Chapter 3). However, she also reported that there was no difference between monolingual and bilingual children on nonverbal tests of intelligence in which problem solutions did not require any verbal knowledge. Yet, somehow, that moderate conclusion did not make its way into the public discourse.

Why were these studies even conducted? There had long been interest in finding a way to measure and compare intelligence across individuals, and scientists in the 19th century came up with a variety of creative approaches. Paul Broca, the eminent neurosurgeon who identified a crucial region of the brain involved in language use that now has his name, took skulls from deceased patients at his hospital, filled them with lead shot, and weighed the filled skull. His argument was that a bigger skull could hold more lead shot and more lead shot indicated that the space had been occupied by a bigger brain. Bigger brains, he assumed, were more intelligent! Around the same time, Francis Galton, who was a first cousin of Charles Darwin, simply measured the size of an individual's head and directly inferred intelligence. In this case, however, the motivation was explicitly sinister: Galton was an enthusiastic member of the new eugenics movement whose mission was to modify the human race through selective parenting. Darwin, it must be noted, strongly disavowed the fraudulent science espoused by his cousin. Unsurprisingly, these crude methods did little to advance the real agenda that was only somewhat hidden, and eventually these studies came to an end. Broca, for example, reluctantly noted that his research found that in some cases German brains were larger than French ones, criminal brains were larger than those of non-criminals, and unintelligent people sometimes had larger brains than professors, so he decided to give up the "delicate subject".

It was a turning point, therefore, when Lewis Terman of Stanford University introduced the Stanford-Binet Test in 1916. It was quickly embraced as a modern, high-tech means of measuring intellectual capacity. Moreover, it had an irresistible scientific veneer: it produced a simple number that was objective and easy to interpret. The items on the test were organized so they became increasingly difficult and therefore less likely to be solved correctly. Since children presumably became smarter as they got older, the point at which the test items became too hard was related to their age. Therefore, an individual's score on the intelligence test, called *mental age*, was compared to the average score expected for a person of that age, called *chronological age*, to create a ratio. The ratio was then multiplied by 100 to produce the individual's Intelligence

Quotient, or IQ. Therefore, anyone performing better than the average for their age had an IQ of over 100, and anyone performing poorer than average for their age had an IQ of less than 100. The intelligence scores for the entire population were presumed to follow a normal distribution, called bell curve because of its distinctive shape, as shown in Figure 3. Intelligence testing rapidly grew into an enormous industry, and tests appeared in every sector of society. However, it is important to understand the dark roots of these tests, a history told in riveting detail by Stephen Jay Gould [105] in his book *The Mismeasure of Man.* According to Gould's account, these new intelligence tests played an oversized role in managing immigration to the United States coming through Ellis Island in the first part of the 20th century.

This was the context in which early bilingualism research used the new IQ tests to measure the possible differences in intellectual ability between monolingual and bilingual children. It was the results of these studies that created the shadow over bilingualism, as they declared that it was harmful to children. However, these tests are problematic for many reasons, beginning with the real possibility that there is no single attribute called "intelligence", and the many factors that impact performance on them, such as socioeconomic status and proficiency in the language of the test, are not accounted for. It should not be surprising, therefore, that most studies reported the negative outcomes described above. But as Darcy recognized in her reviews and described above, the outcomes are different if you are considering verbal tests of intelligence and nonverbal tests of intelligence. In short, bilingual children are neither more nor less intelligent than monolingual children, but their linguistic abilities are different, a point that should surprise no one.

A landmark study in 1962 by two Canadian researchers, Elizabeth Peal and Wallace Lambert, [106] introduced new evidence into the debate and had a profound effect on subsequent research. They used intelligence tests, as had the previous studies, and they framed their predictions around Darcy's conclusions, namely, equivalent performance for nonverbal tests but better performance for monolinguals on verbal tests. However, their dramatic results were that bilingual children outperformed monolingual children on all tests, verbal and nonverbal. This was a major departure from all the previous results. The study led to a reconsideration of the harmful effects of bilingualism and stimulated more research that would inevitably be different from earlier studies. Recall that this was the time when notions of language and thought were changing. But why did Peal and Lambert obtain such different results from earlier IQ studies? One can only speculate, but it is worth noting that these positive results for both verbal and nonverbal measures have not been replicated. The study compared monolingual French-speaking children and French-English bilingual children in Montreal, and it is possible that the social context of the city in 1960, in which the French- and English-speaking communities led quite separate lives and provided limited access to bilingualism, had some influence on the results. These unique features of Montreal are described in more detail elsewhere [107]. To date, the available evidence supports the conclusion of Darcy: no group differences in nonverbal intelligence, but monolinguals typically perform better than bilinguals on verbal tests.

Cognition in the mind

After the cognitive revolution shifted concern in psychology from details of reinforcement schedules to concepts and their representations in mind, questions about the potential impact of experience on cognition could be entertained. Therefore, research after 1962, and especially after around 1980, employed the tools of cognitive psychology to uncover how cognitive processing might differ between monolingual and bilingual children. Within cognitive processing, the most attention since approximately 2000 has been placed on a group of abilities called "executive functions." These are the cognitive processes that we use when problems require attention or planning; for example, in multitasking or carrying out mental calculations. These are problems for which it is necessary to put effort into maintaining focus on the problem, especially if there is competing or distracting information that will interfere with the correct solution. Executive functioning allows you to choose the correct option from a busy set of possibilities and not just settle for the bright shiny distraction. We use executive functions when we drive on a highway and need to focus on the traffic, the exit signs, and road conditions without being distracted by advertisements or fancy cars that suddenly appear in our field of vision. Executive functioning also includes planning and emotional regulation, so the organizing and multitasking required to prepare a complex dinner party (and the subsequent emotional regulation needed to avoid discussion of religion or politics at the table!) require these processes.

Executive function processes are carried out by networks of neurons situated in the front part of the brain, in a region called the frontal lobes (see description in Chapter 6). The frontal lobes are the last brain region to develop in childhood (their development is not in fact complete until late adolescence) and the first to decline with normal aging. Therefore, all the functions controlled by this region should appear late in development and disappear early in aging, and that is exactly what happens with executive functioning. In a very real sense, when your toddler has a meltdown tantrum and seems incapable of responding to reason, part of the problem is that the immaturity of the frontal lobes makes it impossible for the child to control her behavior no matter how much she may want to! It is also why multitasking becomes next to impossible in older age – don't even try it!

The development of executive functions in childhood is the most important cognitive achievement of the child's life. Executive function ability is related to a wide range of cognitive measures, but also predicts academic success, later vocational achievement, and long-term health and well-being [108]. Executive functions matter greatly! An example of these long-term effects comes from the famous "marshmallow test" [109]. Young children are seated in a room with an experimenter and are given a marshmallow. The child is pleased! The experimenter then tells the child he has to go out but will be back soon. Children are told they can eat the marshmallow now if they like, but if they wait until the experimenter returns, they can have two marshmallows instead.

The marshmallow is tempting but waiting offers a better reward. Resisting the lure of the marshmallow requires executive functioning. In the hidden camera videos taken while children are waiting, you can see an incredible range of strategies to help get through the waiting time: children sitting on their hands, pacing the room, turning their back to the marshmallow, playing with their fingers, and sometimes, just eating the marshmallow! The dramatic result was that a 10-year follow-up study showed that children who resisted eating the marshmallow when they were 4 years old were more academically and socially competent, more verbal, and more attentive years later. The control exhibited when children were young predicted a wide range of later achievements.

Once research on the impact of bilingualism followed the lines of cognitive psychology, as opposed to intelligence testing, investigations of the development of executive functioning in monolingual and bilingual children became an active area of research. There was rapid growth in the number of studies, the types of paradigms, and the range of groups tested. It is important to note that these studies did not arise from the earlier intelligence studies, or even from the Peal and Lambert study showing better IQ scores in bilingual children, but rather from those on metalinguistic awareness described in Chapter 4. The evidence showing that bilingual children were better able to ignore distracting meaning and report that "Apples grow on noses" is said the right way says little about their linguistic knowledge or even their IQ; it is evidence for better attention, the key element of executive functioning. In that sense, the "apples" question is as much a test of executive functioning as it is of metalinguistic awareness.

The results of these studies are not simple and they are not entirely consistent, but the majority showed that tasks used to evaluate executive functioning were performed better by bilingual children than by monolinguals [110]. The tasks tend to be simple tests in which an action is carried out in the presence of distractors that need to be ignored, so attention is needed to select the correct choice. For example, a common executive function task is the flanker task for which there is also a variant designed for young children called the fish flanker. In the standard task, the participant sees a row of five arrows (or swimming fish in the children's version) with a response key positioned on each side of the display. The task is to indicate the direction that the middle arrow is pointing (or the direction the middle fish is swimming) by pressing the appropriate response key as quickly as possible without making mistakes. The four flanking arrows (or fish) can be pointing in the same direction as the middle arrow

$$\leftarrow \ \leftarrow \ \leftarrow \ \leftarrow \ \leftarrow$$

creating an easy congruent trial, or in the opposite direction

$$\leftarrow \ \leftarrow \ \rightarrow \ \leftarrow \ \leftarrow$$

creating a more difficult incongruent trial. For the incongruent trials, the participant has to ignore the fact that 80% of the stimuli are providing misleading information. Bilingual children generally outperform monolinguals on this task in that they respond faster and are less distracted by the misleading arrows. To perform this task quickly and accurately, it is necessary to remain focused on the middle arrow and avoid being distracted by the flankers.

Why do we care that bilingual children are faster than monolingual children at pressing a key to indicate the direction of an arrow? One could safely assume that this problem does not come up much in real life, and that the small difference in time that it takes for monolinguals and bilinguals to respond cannot possibly make any real difference to cognitive ability, let alone life. However, this basic ability is at the core of a set of tasks that also rely on executive functioning but are substantially more consequential for cognitive functioning. If bilingual children have better development of these simple executive function abilities, do they also show better development of complex abilities that also rely on executive functioning?

Theory of mind

We assume that other people have minds that work in much the same way as our own and that their behavior can be explained by the beliefs, desires, and intentions that are represented in those minds. When I feel thirsty, I get a drink, so, if I see you get a drink, I assume that you feel thirsty, even though I cannot see into your mind. This understanding that other people have minds and that their content may be different from your own is called theory of mind. You need a theory of mind to understand how other people behave and what the world might look like from a different perspective, especially for someone who has access to different information than you do. Simply put, theory of mind is the recognition that behaviors are caused by mental states, and that those mental states can be different in other people.

The development of theory of mind is a landmark achievement of childhood. The absence or delay of a typically developing theory of mind is associated with such conditions as autism spectrum disorder, schizophrenia, and brain damage, among others. Essentially, having a theory of mind means being able to understand the reasons other people behave the way they do and therefore being able to predict how they will behave, an important social skill. In its simplest form, we make inferences based on connections we know to be true: that is why I assume you are thirsty when I see you taking a drink. But sometimes, the beliefs that motivate other people to act turn out to be incorrect, what are called "false beliefs". If a person holds a false belief, they may act in a way that seems irrational to those who know the true situation. For example, if I decline your offer of a cookie because I believe it has peanut butter to which I am allergic, but you know it does not have peanut butter, you may be baffled by my action. It requires a well-developed theory of mind to figure out the logical implications that follow from someone holding a false belief. This notion is at the center of children's theory of mind.

The tasks used to measure children's understanding of false beliefs ask them to predict how some story character will react in a situation where it has incomplete knowledge of the relevant information. In other words, the scenarios include information that is known by some characters, including the child, but not by others. Therefore, a conflict is set up between what the child knows and what the character knows. The child must distinguish between the information to which she has access, the information to which the other character has access, and the expected behavior that would follow from each.

Just like the simple flanker task, the essence of the false belief task is conflict. In the flanker task, children must pay attention to the middle arrow without being distracted by the flankers. For theory of mind, children must accept that there can be two beliefs that lead to different behaviors. In both cases, the correct choice is the less obvious one, so greater attention is needed to select it. It is arguably more important to understand how behavior is related to mental states, even false mental states, than it is to decide which way an arrow is pointing. Does ability with simple executive function tasks like flanker help bilingual children understand the complex problems involved with false belief?

A common task used to assess children's understanding of false belief is the Sally-Anne task. Children are shown two containers, a box and a basket, and two dolls, Sally and Anne. Then they are told a story about them while the experimenter acts it out with the objects. "Sally and Anne are playing but then Sally has to leave. Sally has a chocolate that she wants to save for later, so before she leaves, she puts the chocolate in the box. (Sally doll leaves.) While she is gone, Anne moves the chocolate from the box to the basket. (Anne carries out the action.) When Sally comes back, where will she look for the chocolate?" The conflict is that the child knows that the chocolate is in the basket, but Sally does not, yet the child must answer from Sally's perspective. To answer correctly, therefore, children must violate what they know to be true and say that Sally will look in the box. Typically developing children can give the correct answer at around 4 years old.

In another false belief task, unexpected contents, the child is shown a familiar package, such as a Smarties box. The experimenter shakes it and asks the child what is inside the box. The child confidently says, "Smarties". The experimenter then opens the box and shows the child that it actually contains pencils. Once it is established that the child knows that the Smarties box contains pencils, the experimenter asks the child what another child who has not seen this demonstration will think is in the box. The solution again depends on understanding that another person who did not see the experimenter open the box will have a false belief about its contents. Until theory of mind is established, children claim that a new child will say that the box contains pencils.

In these and other theory of mind tasks, most studies show that bilingual children provide more correct answers than monolingual children of the same age. This pattern was confirmed in a large meta-analysis that showed that bilingual children were overall better than their monolingual counterparts in performing these tasks [111]. Therefore, despite some studies showing no difference between groups of monolingual and bilingual children, the use of techniques like meta-analysis allows the larger picture to emerge.

Just as false belief is a more compelling and practical demonstration of executive functioning than the flanker task, perspective-taking in communication may be an even more compelling demonstration than false belief. To understand what a speaker is trying to convey, it is necessary to understand the information from the speaker's point of view. This, too, is an aspect of theory of mind. Samantha Fan and colleagues [112] gave a communication task to children who were 4- to 6-years old. The child and the experimenter (speaker) sat on opposite sides of a large 4 x 4 standing grid with objects placed in some of the 16 cells. Therefore, both were looking at this shelving unit from a different perspective. This arrangement is shown in Figure 6. The experimenter asked the child for a particular object and the child had to select the intended target. The trick was that some of the cells had a backing so that only the child could see the object in that cell because it hid the view for the experimenter. The child had to understand that the experimenter could not see the item in some of the cells, and so, needed to select the object that fit the description but was also visible to the experimenter. For example, if the experimenter asked for the "small car", the child needed to select the smallest car that the *experimenter* could see, even if there was a smaller car she could see, hidden from the experimenter. This situation is shown by the single asterisk in Figure 6, where the child can see a small car that the experimenter cannot. Overall, bilingual children were more accurate than monolingual children in selecting the object that took account of the information that was available to the experimenter. There was also a third group of children in this study. They lived in bilingual homes where they were exposed to multiple languages but had not acquired much proficiency in that language, so they were not strictly bilingual. Nonetheless, those children performed just as well as the bilingual ones. The key experience in this case is not necessarily being able to speak another language; instead, having exposure to multiple languages appears to stimulate the development of these difficult concepts by providing an environment that includes variability in expressive forms.

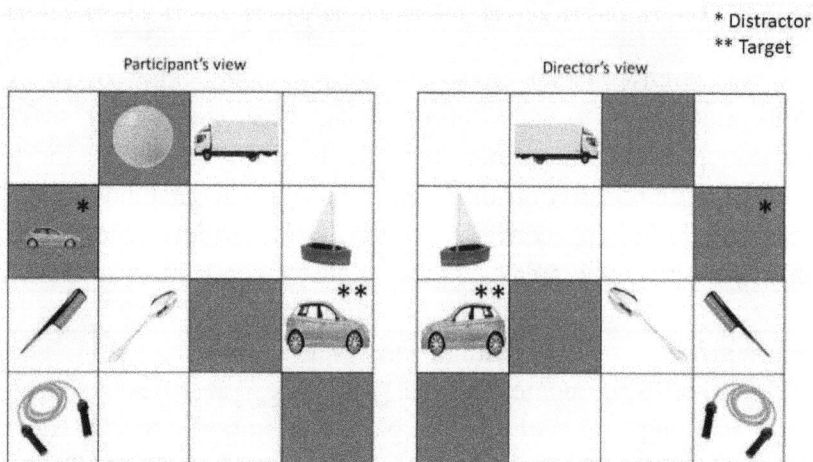

Figure 6. Arrangement of the grid from Fan and colleagues study showing the different views seen by the child (Participant) and experimenter (director). Circle indicates a cell that gives different information to each.

Understanding how beliefs, desires, and intentions determine behavior, and realizing the relation between an individual's beliefs and their perspective is an important childhood development. Achieving that understanding and being able to apply it to actual situations requires all the elements of executive functioning: focused attention, selection, shifting point of view. Across the majority of the research, children who have had the experience of navigating multiple languages achieve these insights more easily.

The Socioeconomic Status (SES) factor

The early research results that showed better performance on executive function tasks by bilingual children than their monolingual peers were surprising, so research groups began to attempt replications of these studies, a normal practice in scientific inquiry. Some of the attempts failed to reveal different performance between the groups, so speculation began as to why that might be the case. One prominent explanation was that the group differences did not actually reflect an impact of bilingualism, but in fact revealed differences in socioeconomic status between the language groups [113]. For this explanation to be correct, it would have to be the case that all the bilingual children in those studies had higher SES than the monolingual children, a situation that seemed unlikely, but the possibility required serious investigation.

SES is the single most important factor in shaping children's development, as discussed previously for language development and literacy acquisition (Chapter 1). Typically, these studies compare children who live in poverty with children in middle-class environments, and it is not surprising that large differences are observed. The effects of SES on development are powerful, so it is important to determine whether it is some residual effect of SES rather than bilingual experience that accounts for the results in the studies of children performing executive function tasks.

The possibility that SES was responsible for the effects attributed to bilingualism has been investigated using a variety of approaches, and all of them have ruled out SES as being the actual reason for the results. In some cases, SES and bilingualism interacted, so the size of the bilingualism effect depended on the child's level of SES. In these studies, there were larger benefits from bilingualism for children at lower levels of SES; that is, children whose development was more compromised by their environments. In a compelling demonstration, Andree Hartanto and colleagues [114] plotted the results from over 18,000 children who completed executive function tasks and who varied widely in SES. Children's performance over these tasks was calculated as a single score for executive control, indicated here as Executive Function. The results are shown in

Figure 7. The horizontal axis is children's SES, with higher SES levels to the right, and the vertical axis is the score over several executive function tasks, with higher scores higher on the axis. Monolingual children are shown by the solid line, and bilingual children by the broken line. Higher SES is associated with better performance because both lines rise as they move to the right. Bilingualism is also associated with better performance because the broken line is always higher than the solid line. But importantly, there is also an interaction effect: bilingualism had a larger impact on improving executive function performance for low SES children who were perhaps at greater developmental risk from their environment than for higher SES children. In this way, bilingualism may compensate for developmental difficulties attributed to environmental factors.

Unlike the research that investigates the impact of SES in which middle-class and low SES children are compared, most of the research on bilingualism has been conducted with middle-class children. Therefore, if there is an influence of SES, it must be more subtle than usually found in studies involving children from a wider range of SES backgrounds. Two studies have addressed this question by dividing middle-class samples into higher and lower groups, even though all children were middle class by usual criteria [115, 116]. The main distinction between these two levels of middle SES was the level of parents' formal education. In both studies, children from the higher SES band performed better than those in the (somewhat) lower SES band, and bilingual children performed better than their monolingual counterparts. Unlike the Hartanto study, there was no interaction between bilingualism and SES, presumably because none of the children were in low SES high-risk groups for which bilingualism could potentially offset potential harm. The studies do, however, point to another environmental factor that is influential in children's development: parents' education level.

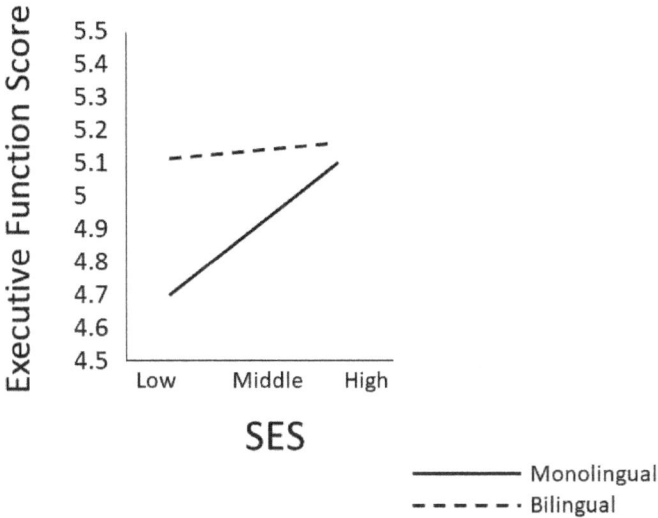

Figure 7. Performance on executive function tasks by 18,200 children from different levels of socioeconomic status. From Hartanto et al. [113]

Finally, two further studies have examined the effect of bilingualism in low SES samples. In these cases, SES is not a factor because all the children share the same demographic, so any differences in bilingualism could not be attributed to SES. In both cases, bilingual children outperformed monolingual children on executive function tasks [59, 117]. SES is always a factor in children's development, but there is no evidence that it explains results demonstrating a beneficial effect of bilingualism on children's performance.

Begin at the beginning

Bilingual children outperform monolingual children on simple executive function tasks like the flanker task, and on complex conceptual problems like theory of mind tasks. On the surface, these appear to be very different types of problems; one can imagine situations in real life that correspond to the ability tested in theory of mind tasks where taking a different perspective is essential, but it is hard to imagine any relevance to figuring out which direction a central arrow is facing. However, there is an important connection between them. In both cases, successful performance requires paying attention to relevant information (the central arrow, the false belief) and ignoring distracting information (the flanking arrows, the child's true belief). In this way, both problems are ultimately based on the ability to focus attention on correct information under challenging conditions, a process sometimes called "selective attention". Attention is fundamental to cognition, and selective attention is particularly integral to executive functioning, but unlike executive functions, attention develops throughout childhood, beginning at birth. It is in this earliest developmental stage that the most exciting research has been produced.

Infancy is the frontier for understanding the origins of the possible effects of bilingual environments on development. It is a surprising place to even consider looking for such effects because babies don't speak! However, in the first year of life, they absorb much about their environment and the language or languages they hear. The first year is also a crucial time for the development of attention and babies' ability to control attention and establish the basic skills of selective attention is well underway.

It may seem improbable that bilingual environments in which more than one language is routinely used affect babies' development, but an important finding described in Chapter 1 makes it at least plausible: In the first year of life, babies in bilingual environments can distinguish between the languages they hear, and they can even detect when a speaker switches from one to the other by looking only at her face with no sound. This ability to discriminate between languages is early evidence for the presence of selective attention: at the very least, they understand that there are two systems. And just as later attention needs to be selectively directed to the middle arrow rather than the peripheral arrows in the flanker task or the child's true belief and the character's false belief in the theory of mind task, infants are learning to choose between two languages. Is it possible that in the first year of life infants in bilingual environments have had enough experience with this type of selective attention to accelerate the development of those processes?

Several studies suggest that this is exactly what happens. Agnes Kovacs and Jacques Mehler [119] gave a learning task to 7-month-old babies. The babies were placed comfortably in a crib and looked at a display positioned above them while an electronic eye-tracker recorded where they were looking. A cue was presented in the center of the display and then an exciting visual image appeared on one side. This visual reward was very motivating, and the babies quickly learned to look to that side as soon as the cue appeared so they could see it sooner. After a set of trials, the protocol was switched so that the reward appeared on the opposite side to the one they had learned to look. After the rule changed, only babies from bilingual environments changed their behavior and attended to the new side. This finding has been replicated in other studies [120]. The linguistic environment in bilingual homes is more complex than that in monolingual homes, so the explanation is that babies in these homes quickly develop attention strategies that are suited to those more variable environments, which results in them having better control over selective attention than is found for infants in monolingual homes [121]. It is compelling evidence that control over attention, and selective attention in particular, may be boosted by babies' early experience in bilingual environments.

Although it is surprising to find cognitive effects of bilingualism in preverbal babies, that is exactly what these studies indicate. The effect is subtle, but these babies show better ability to control their attention in simple perceptual tasks, and control of attention is a foundational aspect of cognitive development. Importantly, these benefits for the development of the attention system do not require using language in any productive way; simple exposure to a bilingual environment can lead to the establishment of distinct linguistic representations, and the presence of distinct representations is an invitation to engage selective attention to navigate the world.

Does bilingualism affect cognition?

Around 30 years ago, a group of researchers claimed that children who listened to Mozart sonatas performed better on a set of cognitive tasks (that were in fact taken from items in the Stanford-Binet intelligence test) than children who did not hear the music, a finding that came to be known as the Mozart Effect [122]. This finding was met with great excitement as it seemed to present a simple intervention to improve children's cognition and led to a small industry of products that were advertised as building on this research to boost children's intelligence. Within a short time, however, it became clear that the effect could not be replicated. Are claims for bilingual effects on cognition another example of the Mozart Effect?

Recall that the early research on bilingualism was based on intelligence test scores, just as was done for the Mozart effect. It is now clear that bilingual experience does not change intellectual capacity: bilingual children are not more or less intelligent than monolingual children. There is, however, evidence that bilingual experience does modify some aspects of children's cognitive processes, and those modifications sometimes enable bilingual children to perform certain tasks better than their monolingual counterparts, or at least, learn how to perform those tasks at an earlier age.

The idea that bilingual experience could modify cognitive ability or executive function was eventually applied to adults, but there, the results were more varied. In many cases, the results showed better performance by bilinguals, but in many other, the results simply showed no difference between groups [123], leading some to argue that the claim for bilingual effects on cognition was unwarranted. However, those studies may have been looking in the wrong place. It turns out that how quickly one performs a flanker task is not a good measure of whether bilingualism has modified cognitive processing, and possibly not an important one either. These tasks are very easy for adults, and all adults perform them extremely fast: on average, in about half a second for each trial. Therefore, not finding group differences on these measures should not be overinterpreted. To make the situation murkier, the decision about who counts as bilingual has been uneven, which possibly has contributed to different results across these studies [124]. However, studies that include various types of neural imaging, such as recording the electrical brain activity or observing patterns of blood flow into different brain regions while participants are performing a task, have consistently shown that regardless of the behavioral outcome, performance is different for monolingual and bilingual individuals [125]. Therefore, the actual effect of bilingual experience on the mind may be in the development, organization, and efficiency of attention systems, particularly selective attention. This is why the earliest appearance of selective attention in infancy is better established for babies in bilingual environments than for those in single language environments, and why several years later, bilingual children become less confused on theory of mind tasks that require their attention to focus on the false belief held by another character, avoiding the salience of their own belief. Bilingual children frequently outperform monolingual children on executive function tasks, but these are often too simple for group differences to appear in adults performing them.

The conclusion from these studies is that bilingual experience changes the way attention is allocated, making it more efficient for bilinguals than monolinguals, and requiring fewer resources to achieve the same performance level. The reason is likely because experience in a complex environment where attention must be divided between two languages provides essential practice in those selective attention processes. Sometimes, this also leads to better performance on tasks, although some studies show no significant group differences. However, the ability to use attention efficiently is extremely important; it means that there are resources in reserve when problems become more challenging. Therefore, even though monolinguals and bilinguals often perform similarly on simple problems, monolinguals begin to struggle as the attention demands of a problem increase, while bilinguals maintain their level of performance. Nevertheless, the real benefit of these honed attention processes appears much later in life, a point we will discuss in Chapter 7.

Take-away conclusions

- Early studies comparing monolingual and bilingual children on intelligence tests reported poor performance by bilingual children, but those results were eventually found to be misleading

- Executive functioning is the most important domain of cognitive development, and bilingual children generally master these tasks earlier or more easily than monolingual children
- The ability that may account for these results is the development of selective attention, something that is more advanced for babies in bilingual environments in the first year of life

Chapter 6
Inside the Bilingual Brain

Bilingual children develop some aspects of language and cognitive abilities differently from monolingual children. Sometimes that development looks more favorable for bilingual children, as in the development of executive functions (Chapter 5), and sometimes it appears more delayed, as in vocabulary development in each language (Chapter 3). Obviously, all our behavior and all children's development happen because of our brains. Do these developmental differences in language and cognition mean that bilingual children have different brains than monolingual children? What happens when we "look under the hood"?

First, let us learn some basic information about the brain. The human brain consists of about 85 billion nerve cells called *neurons* (the stated number used to be around 100 billion, but better imaging methods have recently led to reduced estimates). Neurons make up the *grey matter* of the brain. These neurons communicate with each other, as well as with other cells in the body, by sending electrical signals across microscopic spaces between them called *synapses.* During development, a layer of fatty tissue called *myelin* develops over the neurons creating a coating that protects them. This coating makes up the *white matter* of the brain. The white matter increases the speed and efficiency of the neuronal signals, so they move faster and more accurately. It is the same principle as covering an electrical wire with a rubber coating to make it safer and prevent the signal from escaping from the wire. It takes many years for the myelin to fully develop, and the areas of the brain that have been myelinated function better than those that have not. The three main components of a functioning brain, therefore, are grey matter, white matter, and synapses, and in all cases, more is better.

The final thing to understand is that the brain is roughly divided into four sections or lobes. To some extent, each lobe is primarily specialized for a different function even though all of the brain is somewhat involved in most things we do. The popular idea that we only use 10% (or whatever portion) of our brain is pure fiction. Brain development involves the growth of white matter and the increasing number of (and specialization of) synaptic connections, contributing to grey matter. All these processes generally proceed from the back of the brain to the front, and the frontal lobe is the last to mature. This process is carried out over a very long time: myelination of the frontal lobe is not complete until around 20 years old. Therefore, most of the cognitive processes involved in bilingual processing, and those that best distinguish bilingual cognition from that of monolinguals, like executive functioning, are seated in the frontal lobe. Figure 8 shows an illustration of these brain regions.

Brain scientists typically distinguish between brain structure and brain function. Brain structure refers to the physical state of the organ, usually described in terms of density or volume of grey and white matter. Brain function refers to the connective patterns among the neurons and the brain regions that are used when we engage in a specific activity. Brain function, therefore, is a description of what is happening in the brain at the moment a task is being performed: which neural pathways are used, which brain regions are active. These functional patterns are remarkably consistent across individuals, so we know which pathways we expect to be active when we ask someone to remember a list of words or solve a spatial puzzle. However, they are also modified by specific experiences so that the regions typically used for one task can be "reprogramed" to be used for another. For example, vision is processed in the occipital cortex at the back of the brain (Figure 8), but people who are blind from birth use those brain regions for sound and touch [126]. The human brain is supremely adaptable.

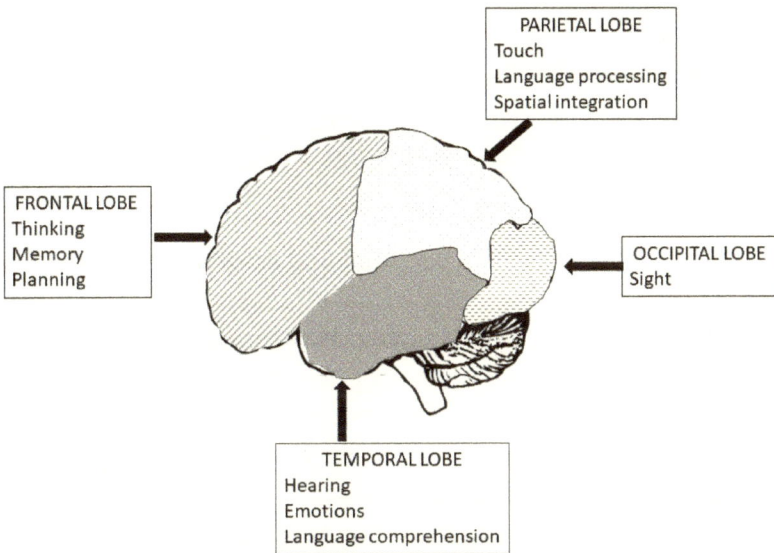

PARIETAL LOBE
Touch
Language processing
Spatial integration

FRONTAL LOBE
Thinking
Memory
Planning

OCCIPITAL LOBE
Sight

TEMPORAL LOBE
Hearing
Emotions
Language comprehension

*Figure 8. Human brain indicating four primary lobes
and several major functions for each.*

Which brings us back to bilingualism. Experience also has the potential to affect brain structure. For example, learning to juggle leads to measurable changes in both grey and white matter structures in the brain, especially in regions specialized for motor control and spatial perception [127]. Bilingualism appears to be another such experience.

In the first major study that compared brain structure for individuals with different language experiences, the researchers found grey matter volume in specific areas of the brain to be greater for bilinguals than for comparable monolinguals, notably in areas involved in language processing [128]. More intriguing, the degree to which this volume was enhanced for bilinguals was related to the degree of bilingual experience; more bilingual experience led to greater volumetric brain changes.

Functional changes have also been found to follow from bilingual experience [129]. Here, too, there are consistent patterns in which various brain regions, particularly those associated with front or back areas of the brain, are employed differently by monolingual and bilingual individuals as discussed below.

Moreover, as with the structural changes described above, the functional brain modifications found in adults are also related to the degree of bilingual experience: more experience is associated with greater changes [130]. This is not surprising, the more you engage in an activity, the more you can expect it to change the underlying structures that power it.

These differences in brain structure and function associated with bilingual experience are *adaptations* in that they emerge from continued experience in managing two language systems. For structural measures, it is generally the case that greater brain volume is better than lesser volume, so differences are easy to interpret. For functional measures, however, there is no simple value judgement that makes one configuration better than the other. However, studies that relate these functional patterns to behavioral outcomes can identify the configurations that are associated with better performance. This research is primarily conducted with adults. There is simply far less known at this time about the role of bilingual experience on brain development in children.

Developing a bilingual brain

The main goal of brain development is to increase grey matter volume by proliferating synaptic connections among neurons (the actual number of neurons does not change) and expand white matter volume and connectivity by accumulation of myelin. Both structural developments lead to a more mature and better functioning brain. Such adaptations can be studied for many experiences, but a unique feature of language experience is that learning a second language can occur at any time, so it is also possible to observe potential differences that bilingual experience might have on brain structure and function in terms of the age at which the child was exposed to bilingualism. This reasoning in which age of exposure is related to the extent of modifications in brain structure is part of the basis for the critical period hypothesis discussed in Chapter 2. Although that argument rests more on brain function than brain structure, brain structure was central to the initial formulation of the argument, which claimed that foreign language learning after puberty was never fully successful because the brain became less adaptable. As we now know, however, the brain remains adaptable throughout life.

As we saw in Chapter 5, the use of brain size in the 19th century to indicate the intelligence of different groups was a dark and misguided exercise, in part because of the nefarious motives of those who conducted those studies, but more importantly because there is no systematic relation between brain size and intelligence in adult humans. However, that is not the case for children whose brains are developing: it is an extremely serious matter if a child's brain volume is restricted because of developmental circumstances, and the implications of that reduced brain volume are found across every aspect of behavior.

There are several biological conditions that delay brain development in children, including such genetic disorders as Down syndrome and phenylketonuria. These are serious conditions that can be traced to specific genetic mutations. There are few successful interventions to tackle them. Environmental conditions can also delay brain development in children, and unlike these genetic mutations, environments can be changed. Just as with cognitive development discussed in Chapter 5, the single most important environmental factor that impacts brain structure development in children is socioeconomic status (SES). The failure of brain structure to develop normally affects all aspects of children's lives —emotional, cognitive, academic, social— and a substantial body of research has demonstrated a relation between SES and brain volume [131]. We have already seen that bilingualism can interact with SES to mitigate the most serious consequences of low SES on cognitive performance. Can it have similar effects on developing brain volume?

Some evidence for this possibility comes from a large-scale study of approximately 600 children in which grey matter volume, indicated by cortical surface area, was compared for monolingual and bilingual children [132]. The children covered a wide range of ages, from 3- to 20-years old, and lived in various SES environments as indicated by parents' education and income. This information was used to simply divide the sample into two groups, high or low, that could then be related to the two language groups, monolingual or bilingual. The questions, therefore, were whether high or low SES was associated with different brain volumes, whether monolingual or bilingual language experience was associated with different brain volumes, and whether there was an interaction between those factors. The answer was "yes" to all three questions, and the results were similar to those found in the large-scale study of executive function abilities conducted by Hartanto and colleagues described in Chapter 5. In the case of this brain study, there was no difference in cortical volume between monolingual and bilingual children in the higher SES group, but there were substantial differences between language groups for children in the low SES group. Specifically, for children living in low SES environments where brain development was at risk from these social circumstances, the bilingual children had substantially more developed brain volume than their monolingual counterparts. These dramatic results are shown in Figure 9. As with the results from the cognitive tasks, the greatest benefit of bilingual experience is for those who are most in need of additional stimulation. Bilingualism was able to mitigate some of those harmful effects.

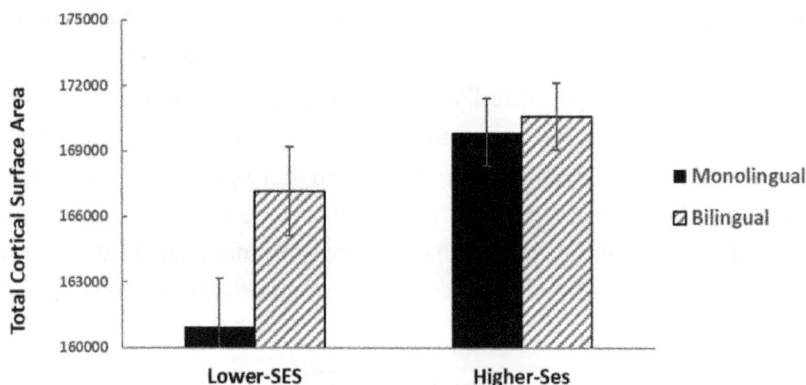

Figure 9. Differences in cortical surface area between monolingual and bilingual children aged 3- to 20-years old from high and low SES groups. Adapted from Brito & Noble [131].

It is also possible to measure grey matter volume in adults and then extrapolate to the effects of bilingualism on brain structure in children. In one such study, grey matter volume was assessed for bilingual adults who were all equally proficient in both languages but had become bilingual at different ages. Those individuals who had been bilingual from birth had more grey matter volume in several relevant brain areas than those who became bilingual later in life [133]. There were no monolinguals in this study, but the results support the claim that these enhanced areas of grey matter were related to the extent of bilingual experience beginning in childhood.

Equally important to grey matter volume is white matter volume and connectivity. White matter allows the brain to communicate effectively by protecting the axon along which the electrical signal is sent. In a study comparing white matter structure in monolingual and bilingual children who were 8- to 11-years old, the authors reported significantly better white matter structure for the bilingual children than for the monolinguals [134], a difference that was sustained over the next several years as these children were followed longitudinally [135]. Recall that white matter continues to develop until around 20 years old, so the bilingual children indicated more advanced accumulation of white matter throughout much of their development.

Together, these studies demonstrate that both grey and white matter are developing better in the brains of bilingual children than in monolinguals, with greater differences for children in low SES environments where brain development is at greater risk. Combining these results, Christos Pliatsikas and colleagues [136] examined both grey and white matter in a large sample of approximately 700 children and confirmed that for both structures, there was more robust development in bilingual children than in monolinguals. In the case of brain function, which we discuss in the next section, it is not possible to claim that one organizational system is better than another, but in the case of brain structure, more is pretty much always better.

Organizing the brain to function

All the activities of our brain are carried out by connected networks in the brain: the "functional organization" that reflects how we use our brains to achieve our intended goals. Although there are standard functional patterns associated with specific activities, there are also variations in those patterns. We begin, then, with the simplest question: Do monolingual and bilingual children recruit different brain networks when using language? The question is simple because current neuroimaging techniques, such as functional magnetic resonance imaging (fMRI) track which brain regions are recruited in real time while an individual is performing a task. It is also simple because it is the domain most likely to reveal a difference: It would not be surprising that language processing is handled differently by people who speak one or more than one language. These differences have already been reported for adult monolinguals and bilinguals. More interesting, however, is that the nature and extent of these differences in brain region recruitment for language processing depends on the age at which the person becomes bilingual [137]. In general, later acquisition of a second language is associated with recruitment of a broader range of brain regions, whereas early acquisition, as in bilingualism from birth, shows less difference from monolingual patterns. One way of explaining this pattern is that the adaptation is more effortful or extensive for languages learned later in life.

A well-known popular dictum is that language is processed in the left side of the brain. That is largely true, although the extensions of this notion to include descriptions of "left brain" and "right brain" individuals who differ in talent, temperament, and personality are almost certainly false. Like everything we do, language uses the entire brain, but the most important processing regions are indeed in the left hemisphere, and more specifically, in the left inferior frontal gyrus. A less technical way of putting that idea is to say that the functional networks for language processing are housed in lower left regions of the brain.

So, do monolingual and bilingual children process language differently? In a series of studies using a non-invasive imaging technology called functional near-infrared spectroscopy (fNIRS), functional brain organization was measured while monolingual and bilingual children performed various language tasks. The purpose was to determine if children in the two groups were using similar or different brain networks while performing these verbal tasks. In one study, children were asked to make linguistic judgments about sentences (see for example grammaticality judgment tasks described in Chapters 2 and 4), and the results showed that bilingual children used more tightly-clustered and focused networks in left hemisphere language networks than the monolinguals [138]. This is interesting because it is consistent with other research showing that greater skill is associated with more focused, or less extensive brain activation. In general, younger adults perform tasks using fewer brain regions than older adults performing the same tasks [139]. Even very specific skills, such as car racing, are carried out with less extensive, that is more focal activation, by professional race car drivers than non-drivers [140]. In the fNIRS studies described here, monolinguals and bilingual had similar language proficiency, but the functional activation patterns showed more focal processing of that knowledge by the bilinguals. The authors interpret this finding as showing that the bilingual brains show more specialization for language, an outcome that may reflect enriched linguistic experiences. This pattern of more activation in language-related brain regions while performing a linguistic task for bilinguals than monolinguals has also been demonstrated in adults [141].

In an extension of the study investigating functional activation during language processing described above, Maria Arredondo and colleagues used fNIRS to study brain activation in children 7- to 13-years old while they performed a nonverbal executive function task, namely the flanker task described in Chapter 5 [142]. As in previous research, bilingual children performed this task somewhat better than the monolingual children, although the difference in this case was small, presumably because the sample size was also small. These tasks are performed by recruiting networks in the frontal lobe because that is where executive function processes are housed. However, the recruitment of the frontal lobe networks was different for the two language groups: bilingual children relied predominantly on left frontal lobe activation and monolingual children relied more on right frontal lobe activation. Therefore, from childhood, the functionality of the left hemisphere, extending to the frontal lobes, is modified by bilingual experience.

This specialization in which language processing takes place in left hemisphere regions is present even in babies. As we saw in Chapter 5, babies being raised in bilingual environments responded differently to a simple attention task than babies from monolingual environments in that they showed better attentional control. Is it possible that bilingual experience also changes the functional patterns of language perception in infancy?

To investigate that question, Evelyne Mercure and colleagues [143] measured brain activation networks using fNIRS in 60 babies between the ages of 4- and 8-months to determine how they respond to language. The key manipulation was that the babies belonged to one of three groups with very different language experiences: they came from (a) monolingual English environments, (b) bilingual environments that included English and another spoken language, or (c) bimodal bilingual environments that consisted of spoken English and British Sign Language. In this last group, the babies had normal hearing, but there was at least one deaf adult in the house, so sign language was a primary form of communication from the time of their birth. All babies were presented with both spoken and sign language while brain activity was recorded. For all of them, the presentation of spoken English was accompanied by activation in both left and right hemispheres, including the standard left-lateralized language regions, and the presentation of sign language produced activation in the right hemisphere. These general findings make sense, but more detailed analyses indicated different degrees of right- and left-hemisphere involvement for the three groups. The greatest differences in functional separation between the two hemispheres were found for the babies from bilingual environments, while the monolingual and bimodal babies were more similar to each other. The researchers concluded that the unimodal bilingual experience of hearing two spoken languages has greater impact on early brain lateralization than the bimodal bilingual experience. These small differences set out the foundation on which language will evolve over the next few years and indicate that these basic functional structures have already been shaped by language experience in the first year of life.

The differences uncovered in this study are small and may seem trivial. Does it really matter if the left or right brain hemisphere is more involved when listening to language, especially for preverbal babies? All of these babies would grow up to be successful native speakers of English. It might be the case, though, that these small differences are evidence that something more important is taking place in the first year that may indeed impact language abilities throughout life.

International adoption is a prevalent practice in which babies born into precarious conditions, such as girls in China under the one-child policy, are adopted by families in other countries, typically Western countries. The children are raised as members of the new family and learn the new language like any other child, but is there any trace of their early exposure to their home language?

The evidence suggests that the early exposure to the language of birth remains part of their brain organization. In a compelling test of this idea, adolescents (about 13 years old) who had been adopted from China by French-speaking families in Canada were compared to children who came from bilingual homes in which both Chinese and French were spoken, and to monolingual French-speaking children [144]. The adoptees were an average of 12 months old when they were adopted, and after arriving in Canada had no further exposure to Chinese. A unique feature of Chinese is that tone carries important meaning, so attending to it and discriminating among similar sounding tones is an essential aspect of language proficiency because tone determines meanings. As such, there is an identifiable neural signature to tone perception for those familiar with Chinese. The difference is in fact completely sensible: for speakers of non-tonal languages, tone is processed in the right hemisphere like any other auditory stimulus, but for speakers of tonal languages, tone is processed in the left hemisphere because it contains linguistic information. The study showed that both the adoptees from China and the Chinese-French bilinguals processed tone in the same way in the left hemisphere, but the French monolinguals did not. Early experience with this very specific linguistic feature in the first year of life continued to influence functional networks for processing speech more than a decade after they had last been exposed to the language.

The brain in the classroom

The changes in brain structure and function that we have discussed here can be related to the language and cognitive outcomes described in previous chapters. Beyond those achievements, however, children also develop academic skills in schools that build from these foundations. If we accept the rather simple premise that brain structure and brain function underlie all aspects of a child's cognitive development, then perhaps there are organizational differences to be found between monolingual and bilingual children dealing with academic tasks.

A small number of studies have addressed this possibility. Several of them focus on the acquisition of literacy for young children or reading fluency in older children. Although literacy is obviously a language skill and is central to language proficiency, it is also an academic skill in that it is typically learned through instruction, unlike spoken language proficiency which can be mastered through simple exposure. The common conclusion from these studies is that the neural recruitment of brain regions, or the functional organization underlying reading, is different for monolingual and bilingual children. Different functional patterns have been demonstrated for children at different ages [145] and for speakers of different languages learning to read other languages [146]. In this last example, children who were 6 to 10 and were learning to read in one or two languages belonged to one of three groups: (a) monolingual English speakers, (b) Spanish-English bilinguals, or (c) French-English bilinguals. The children read words (bilinguals in both languages) while brain networks were recorded using fNIRS. The two non-English languages have different sound-symbol relations. Spanish is transparent and regular (the same letter always makes the same sound), and French is closer to English in that it is less transparent and includes more irregular words. These differences in the predictability of the writing systems showed up as differences in the brain networks that were recruited to read each language. Bilingual children learning to read in both languages need to use both sets of networks, and their brains must have the flexibility to respond as necessary. As before, it is impossible to place a value on these differences and declare that one configuration is "better" than another, but the presence of different organizational structures points to the impact of bilingual experience at the most profound level of development, namely, the brain.

Because language is the basis for all classroom activity, it might also be the case that monolingual and bilingual children experience non-language subjects differently because they use brain regions differently. In a very old study that became part of the evidence warning parents about the dangers of bilingualism, Macnamara [147] reported that children who were educated through a second language performed more poorly on mathematics measures than did monolingual children educated in their only language. Closer examination of those results, however, revealed that the poorer performance was only found on word-based problems, not on mathematical operations, and that children's proficiency in the language of instruction was actually quite poor. More interesting, therefore, would be evidence that children are recruiting different functional networks while learning mathematics because of their language experiences.

A study by Mondt and colleagues investigated this possibility by examining 8- to 11-year-old children solving mathematical problems while brain activation was recorded using fMRI [148]. All the children were very proficient in both French and Dutch, but there were differences among them in terms of which language they used at school and which one they used at home. The relevant comparison was between those who performed the mathematics task in their school language and those who performed it in their home language. Because mathematics is primarily a school-based activity, it should be processed more efficiently if the problem is presented in the language of schooling. All children received very high accuracy scores, with no difference between groups who were solving the problems in either the school language or the home language. The key result, however, was that children in both groups recruited similar brain networks to perform the mathematical operations, but those who were given the problem in the school language showed significantly less activation than did those in the home language group. This difference in the intensity of brain activation is the signature of efficiency: the same processes can be carried out, to the same level of accuracy, with less effort. These results are similar to those described above showing more focal, that is, less extensive activation for experts than for non-experts.

The emerging structural properties and functional organization of children's brains in early childhood, beginning in infancy, permeate throughout development. Even when these differences do not lead to observable performance effects, or clear indications of better or worse judgments, they speak to the resources that children are developing that will take them through life. Sometimes, as we will see in Chapter 7, it may in fact take a lifetime for the consequences to reveal themselves.

Take-away conclusions

- In some cases, such as low socioeconomic status, bilingual experience can compensate for reduced brain development and produce more rapid growth of grey matter
- Monolingual and bilingual children often use different brain regions when performing the same tasks
- The organization of the brain in terms of which regions are used for specific functions appear to emerge very early and reflect the types of languages encountered in the babies' home

Chapter 7
Aging Bilinguals

It is an inevitable if somewhat depressing fact that aging is accompanied by a slowing down of all our functions, including cognitive ones. Well-known cognitive failures, such as being unable to remember names or where we left our keys are only the most obvious indications of a system that is less sharp and less flexible than it was in younger age. This decline is a normal part of healthy aging and affects all of us, even in the absence of neuropathology, dementia, or other clinical conditions.

Accompanying the well-known memory failures of aging is a decline in executive functioning. As described in Chapter 6, the frontal lobes where the executive functions are housed are the first region of the brain to lose volume with aging. As that erosion of grey matter takes place, the jobs carried out by those regions, notably executive functioning, become increasingly difficult. In almost a reversal of development, aging reduces the structures developed slowly in childhood and decreases access to these high-value executive function processes: last in, first out. So, if bilingual experience propelled the development of those functions in childhood through experience in selective attention with two languages, does ongoing bilingual experience throughout life also slow their decline in older age? Can lifelong bilingual experience protect executive functioning and other cognitive systems against the challenges of aging?

Finding ways to preserve cognition in older age is a major concern for individuals, a priority for government and social institutions, and a scientific focus for many researchers. The available drug treatments that are used to help people experiencing cognitive decline and dementia have limited effectiveness. The ubiquitous advertisements for non-prescription supplements to increase cognitive and memory ability in the healthy population are not well supported by scientific evidence. Until recently, there were no promising pharmacological treatments for Alzheimer's disease currently under investigation [149]. A drug approved in the United States in 2021, called aducanumab, is currently mired in controversy and not approved anywhere outside the U.S. The best alternative at present is to harness the power of a concept called "cognitive reserve": the idea that stimulating activity and mental engagement allows the mind to function even if neuropathology has begun to accumulate [150].

Engaging in activities associated with cognitive reserve builds extra "mental fuel" as cognitive and brain functions are depleted. In that sense, cognitive reserve provides a sort of back-up system that protects cognition despite decreasing brain function. This protection boosts cognitive levels both for individuals experiencing normal healthy aging and for those who are also dealing with disease pathology. Experiences that contribute to cognitive reserve include having more years of formal education, maintaining active social networks and interactions, and engaging in aerobic exercise. People who participate in these activities have better cognitive functions than similar people who do not. Therefore, more cognitive reserve is associated with better cognitive functioning and less severe cognitive decline. We have already seen that bilingualism is a stimulating experience that accelerates children's development. Can it also contribute to cognitive reserve and slow cognitive decline in older age?

The case for cognitive reserve

The normal decline of our cognitive abilities with healthy aging is a source of great frustration. These lapses make themselves known almost daily through simple acts of forgetting (What was his name? Where's the thing that I use to turn over the eggs? What was that movie about the war where the underground fighters met in a bar, there was a piano, something about Sam?) and, as described earlier, failures in executive functioning, such as no longer being able to multitask. (Strictly speaking, no one can ever multitask; the term is a shorthand for juggling two things at the same time and rapidly switching between them, a supreme feat of executive functioning.) There suddenly comes a point in aging when young people all speak too quickly, and everything takes slightly longer to do. Throughout the lifespan, there is a tight correlation between the state of brain structure and the level of cognitive activities that can be expected. This is clear in childhood, as children's brains develop, they become able to take on new and more complex cognitive functions. And typically, in older age, as brains deteriorate with the normal aging process, certain cognitive functions become more difficult. This correlation makes perfect sense if we believe that the cognitive skills that we can carry out are related to the brain resources on which they rely. This correlation between brain state and cognitive level is a recognition of the deep link between our brains and our minds and how they change over the lifespan.

The idea behind cognitive reserve is that this connection can be severed so that cognitive level is no longer tied to brain structure. In short, individuals with more cognitive reserve can outperform the limits imposed by their brain structure [151]. In typical aging, it is possible to predict cognitive level from brain structure because of their strong correlation. This pattern is shown in the left panel in Figure 10 for Typical Aging. The horizontal axis is age, with older ages to the right, and the vertical axis is level for each of brain structure and cognitive performance. Because they are correlated, they decline at the same rate, so as brain structures decay, cognitive levels decline. With cognitive reserve, these levels for brain and cognition become dissociated and it is no longer possible to predict one from the other. This situation is shown in the right panel in Figure 10. In this case, cognitive level remains high despite the deterioration of brain structure.

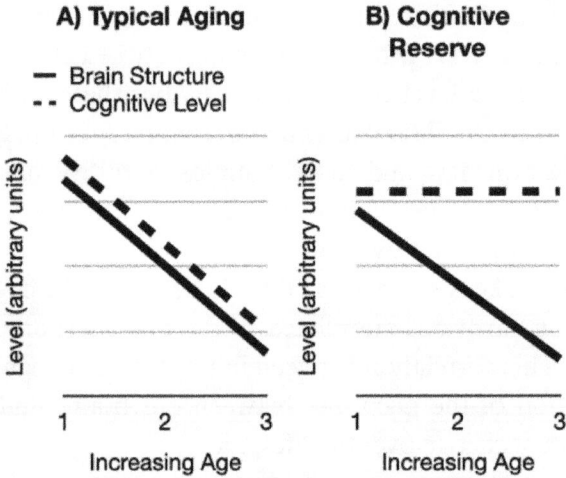

A) Typical Aging

— Brain Structure
- - Cognitive Level

B) Cognitive Reserve

Level (arbitrary units)

1   2   3
Increasing Age

Level (arbitrary units)

1   2   3
Increasing Age

Figure 10. Relation between cognitive level and brain structure with typical aging or cognitive reserve. Reprinted from [150].

The mechanism behind cognitive reserve is "neural plasticity." This notion is based on the very simple idea that repeated experience performing a particular activity changes how that activity is carried out. If we spend a lot of time practicing tennis serves, we get better at executing them. In addition, our brains and muscles responsible for those serves become accustomed to the complex movements and can execute a serve with less effort. In a real sense, the brain has changed, although the effect of that change is very limited and probably only relevant when playing tennis. But the same mechanism applies to cognitive activities. Bilingual experience requires ongoing attention to manage the two languages, as described in Chapter 1, and this use of attention networks changes them, making a range of attention-related activities less effortful. To the extent that these attention-demanding cognitive activities can be executed with less effort, there are more resources left over for other activities. There is more "reserve".

Cognitive reserve is defined in terms of the *relation* between brain structure and cognitive level and not by the absolute value of just one of these. Therefore, investigating the presence of cognitive reserve is more demanding than simply recording brain volume or measuring cognitive level because it requires the consideration of both components. However, few studies on aging do that. Most studies focus on the cognitive side and compare how well monolingual and bilingual older adults perform the types of executive function tasks described earlier. As with young adults, the evidence is mixed, but most studies with older adults report better performance by the bilingual group on these tasks. This is important information but, on its own, it does not support the central feature of cognitive reserve, namely, a disconnect between brain structure and cognitive level. It is only when behavioral and brain evidence are integrated that the picture becomes more informative and addresses the issue of cognitive reserve.

Studies that combine a standard executive function task, such as the flanker task, with some form of neuroimaging can provide information not only on "how well" each group performed the task but also "how" they performed it. With both types of information, it is possible to determine if the relation between them is similar across groups. Using this approach, it has been shown that even when monolingual and bilingual older adults perform a task to the same level of speed or accuracy, they achieve that performance using different processes. Electrophysiological recordings (EEG) indicate how difficult or effortful the task is, and here studies have shown that monolinguals and bilinguals who achieve the same outcome nonetheless reveal that the bilinguals require less "effort" [125]. The EEG signal indicates how much electrical brain activity is needed to carry out a mental function, so examining these recordings provides a precise measure of effort. Similarly, functional magnetic resonance imaging (fMRI) identifies the regions or networks in the brain used to perform the task. These studies indicate that monolinguals and bilinguals use different brain regions while carrying out executive function tasks [152]. The fMRI measures can also show how *much* activation is needed, so, like EEG, less activation indicates that the task required less effort.

A more complete description of how monolingual and bilingual older adults experience aging comes from comparing brain structure across participants in the two groups. These comparisons are particularly useful if the cognitive level of all participants is known and is controlled to be the same for both groups. An important index of brain health is grey matter density, or the volume of neurons in the cortex (see Chapter 6). Although the idea to compare brain volume for the two groups is straightforward, the results are complex. Several studies have carried out these comparisons for monolingual and bilingual healthy older adults who perform at the same level on cognitive tasks, but the results differ across experiments. In one group of studies, bilingual older adults (approximately 60 years old) had greater grey matter volumes than monolinguals [153, 154]; in another group of studies, bilingual and monolingual older adults (65-70 years old) had comparable grey matter volumes [155, 156]; and in a third group, it was the monolingual older adults who had better grey matter volume than the bilinguals (approximately 75 years old) [157]. An illustration of these data showing the crossover effects for older adults is shown in Figure 11. At 60 years old, the bilingual participants have more grey matter volume than monolinguals, but across studies, that volume declines more rapidly than it does for monolinguals shown by a steeper slope, leaving bilinguals with poorer brain structure by 75 years old. How is this possible?

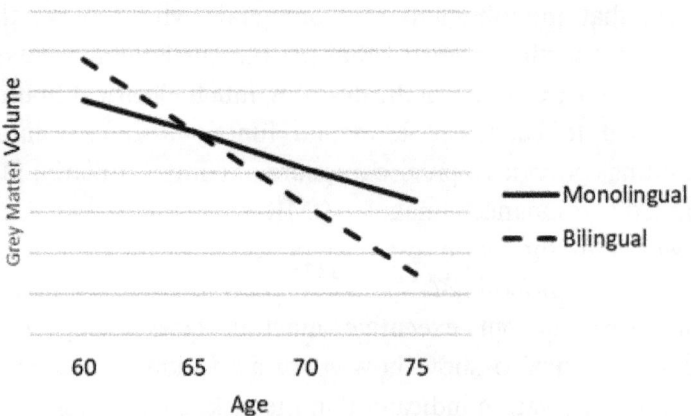

Figure 11. Changes in grey matter volume for monolingual and bilingual older adults over age, based on results from several studies.

The key to understanding these apparently contradictory results is found in thinking about the different age groups examined in these studies. Two main points need to be emphasized. The first is that all the participants were reported to be experiencing healthy aging; none of them had been diagnosed with clinical cognitive decline. In all the studies, participants completed cognitive tasks, and did so to similar performance levels. The second is that gray matter volume declines steadily over the 15 years under consideration for both groups, but that decline is different for monolinguals and bilinguals in these studies. In the youngest group, the bilinguals have more gray matter volume than monolinguals. As the participants become older, the greater brain volume shown by bilinguals in the youngest group decreases more rapidly with age than in the monolinguals, so in the oldest group it is the monolinguals who have more brain volume. These changes, however, are only the latest in a lifelong transformation process in grey matter. Younger bilingual adults, beginning at around 25, have more robust grey matter than their monolingual counterparts [158]. It appears that around 65, the entry point into "older age", things begin to change, and the bilinguals lose ground against the monolinguals. There is a short period of time where levels are largely equivalent for the two language groups, but as age increases, the brain volume of the bilinguals falls below that for monolinguals [159].

On its own, this pattern is disconcerting for bilingualism: Does bilingual experience lead to less healthy brains? Does bilingualism cause brain atrophy? Why is the decline with age in Figure 11 steeper for bilinguals than for monolinguals? Remember that the participants in all these studies were at the same cognitive level, they performed equivalently on all cognitive and experimental tests that were administered, and none of them were experiencing cognitive impairment. It is only brain volume that was different. That means that bilinguals somehow managed to maintain normal cognitive levels *despite* faster deteriorating brains.

To be included in the studies from which these results were extracted, all the participants needed to demonstrate that they were healthy, independently living older adults without cognitive or memory impairment. The possibility, therefore, is that bilinguals can continue to meet this criterion even if brain structure declines, whereas monolingual individuals with compromised brains would no longer be experiencing healthy aging and so would not be eligible for these studies. In other words, bilinguals were able to participate in the studies even after there had been substantial decline in gray matter volume whereas monolinguals with that level of brain volume would fail to meet the criteria for the studies in question.

To test this idea, we conducted a theoretical "brain swap". The question was to determine how monolinguals would manage if they had brains at the level of the bilinguals. We took a group of bilinguals from a previous study who were on average 74 years old. These bilinguals had performed equivalently to monolinguals on a set of cognitive tasks but had poorer brain structure [157]. We then matched the brain structure of those bilinguals to a new set of monolinguals from a large international data base to select a group of individuals who were the same age, sex, and had the same education background as the bilinguals. So, now we had two groups of older adults who had essentially the same brains and the same backgrounds but different language experiences. We knew that 100% of the bilinguals were cognitively normal because that was the criterion for participating in the study in the first place, but what was the cognitive profile of the monolinguals who essentially had the "same brains" as the bilinguals in the previous study? In the monolingual group, 41% of the participants had been diagnosed with clinical cognitive impairment, either mild cognitive impairment or Alzheimer's disease [160]. What is happening, therefore, is that monolinguals whose brain structure is as poor as bilinguals are not eligible to participate in these studies of healthy aging because their cognitive levels have already declined. This is illustrated in the Typical aging panel of Figure 10. Bilingual older adults, in contrast, can function at normal cognitive levels longer than monolinguals because even as brain deterioration occurs, cognition is not affected, as shown in the Cognitive Reserve panel of Figure 10. This pattern illustrates the concept of cognitive reserve.

When cognition fails

Everyone knows someone who is now or has in the past suffered from dementia. It is a devastating illness. The term "dementia" is a general cover that includes many varieties of conditions that can be quite different from each other. Some are associated with other specific diseases, such as Lewy Body Dementia that is related to Parkinson's Disease, and Frontotemporal Dementia that is primarily revealed through difficulties with language and changes in behavior. However, the one that is the most prevalent, most well-known, and arguably most feared, is Dementia of the Alzheimer's Type, or more simply, Alzheimer's Disease. Most of the discussion here will focus on this variety.

The cause of Alzheimer's disease is unknown; although much is known about how it affects brains and cognition, how it progresses, and what impact it has on other physical and cognitive systems, the triggering events remain a mystery. It is possible that solving this mystery will accelerate the search for treatment and possibly even a cure, but at present, there is simply no single identifiable cause. However, there are risk factors that are known to increase the likelihood that an individual will develop this form of dementia. There are genetic variants that predispose some individuals to a particularly virulent form of Alzheimer's disease that often appears at a relatively young age. Some lifestyle factors, such as smoking and poor diet, and health factors, such as high blood pressure and diabetes, also increase the risk of developing Alzheimer's disease, although again, none of these is itself a cause. However, it is also accepted that cognitive reserve factors can provide some protection against Alzheimer's disease; people with more formal education have a lower risk of developing dementia than those will less education. We have seen that bilingualism appears to be a source of cognitive reserve. Does it also provide protection against Alzheimer's disease?

The first study to consider this question took a somewhat indirect approach. If bilingualism offered some protection against dementia, then lifelong bilinguals should be able to cope with the early neuropathology better than monolinguals. In this case, they would not show symptoms in the early stages of the disease. Recall that in healthy aging, bilingual older adults can maintain normal cognition despite evidence for deterioration in brain structure, whereas monolinguals with comparable brain structure had a greater likelihood of being diagnosed with clinical dementia. Extending that argument, bilinguals should be less likely to show the telltale cognitive symptoms of dementia in the early stages so the disease would go undetected. Therefore, in the earliest stages, there would be more diagnoses for monolinguals than for bilinguals.

To test this idea, we examined the records of patients from a memory clinic in a geriatric hospital located in a highly diverse city where approximately half the population is bilingual. For this reason, about half the patients who come to the clinic are also bilingual. This allowed us to match patients so that monolinguals and bilinguals were similar on education and other relevant background measures. Our interest was in the age at which the patients first showed symptoms of dementia and were eventually diagnosed. For both first appearance of symptoms and formal clinical diagnosis, the bilingual patients were significantly older, in fact, around four years older [161]. This delay in onset for bilinguals has now been replicated in clinics in many countries around the world, confirming that bilinguals can cope with early stages of dementia better than monolinguals. The pattern across these studies has been verified using the techniques of meta-analysis that can evaluate the results of a large number of studies [162, 163].

In the earlier discussion of our studies of healthy aging, we showed that bilingual older adults had more deteriorated brains than monolinguals, but similar cognition (see Figure 11). Does the same pattern apply to monolingual and bilingual patients with Alzheimer's disease? If so, we would expect that patients who appear to be at similar clinical levels of dementia may in fact be coping with different degrees of disease. This is exactly what the evidence shows. For monolingual and bilingual Alzheimer's disease patients who are matched on clinical disease level, the bilingual patients have more brain atrophy [164] and poorer glucose metabolism [165, 166], both markers of the degree of disease pathology. In other words, bilinguals were able to cope with more disease than monolinguals at the same level of clinical symptoms. This means that the later detection of the disease in bilinguals came at a more advanced level of disease than was the case for monolinguals. However, while the disease remained undetected, the bilinguals were living independent and unimpaired lives.

Because Alzheimer's disease is a disease of aging, postponing onset of the disease is logically associated with a lower incidence: older individuals will die of something else before symptoms of the underlying Alzheimer's disease become apparent. However, this delay is important because the years during which there is no cognitive impairment despite underlying pathology can be lived independently with a good quality of life. Models based on data for disease incidence predict that a one year delay in symptom onset would reduce worldwide prevalence of Alzheimer's disease in 2050 by approximately 9 million cases, and a delay of 2 years would decrease prevalence by 22 million cases [167].

The evidence showing that bilinguals can tolerate some degree of Alzheimer's pathology before experiencing symptoms of the disease leads to an intriguing possibility: do countries with more bilingual populations have a lower incidence of Alzheimer's disease than countries that are more monolingual? Testing this idea with empirical evidence is immensely difficult. Populations are inherently diverse, making national descriptions such as "monolingual" or "bilingual" questionable at best. Countries also differ in the degree and type of treatment they offer for dementia patients, largely reflecting differences in national wealth and health care support systems. And finally, countries also differ in overall life expectancy, which makes those with longer life expectancy likely to record more dementia cases regardless of language use patterns in the population simply because more people have lived long enough to succumb to the disease. All these factors affect disease prevalence.

One study has attempted to answer this question and controlled as much as possible for all these complicating variables. Raymond Klein and colleagues [168] created a score indicating the mean number of languages spoken by individuals in 93 countries. They also obtained information about the prevalence of Alzheimer's disease in each country from the World Health Organization. The researchers then controlled for factors such as wealth and life expectancy to compare the incidence of Alzheimer's disease across countries that vary in population bilingualism. For countries with a low life expectancy, the incidence of Alzheimer's disease was low and unaffected by any of the tested factors: essentially people did not live long enough to acquire the disease. However, in countries with a medium or long-life expectancy, there was a significant negative relation between bilingualism and disease prevalence: countries with more bilingual populations had lower disease prevalence. This relation was strongest for countries with a long-life expectancy where the likelihood of suffering from Alzheimer's disease was largest. Therefore, the highest prevalence of Alzheimer's disease was in countries that had a long-life expectancy and were largely monolingual. Comparable countries that were more bilingual had significantly less disease prevalence. This is only one study, but the possibilities it raises are compelling.

After the fall

Once dementia has taken hold, there is little that can be done to halt or reverse the course of the disease. However, not all patients experience similar decline. Is there any role for protective factors in buffering the rate at which the disease progresses? This, too, is difficult to track. In a few studies in which we studied monolingual and bilingual patients with Alzheimer's disease, we had pieces of evidence for cognitive level over time [161, 169]. These analyses showed no difference in the cognitive change between patients in the monolingual and bilingual groups, but the data were incomplete, and the assessments not sufficiently controlled. So, the possibility for differences in rate of decline remained unanswered.

The prediction about which patient group will experience more rapid decline turns out to be counterintuitive. For studies comparing first symptoms of evidence for the disease and for those addressing the degree of neuropathology in the early stages, the protective effects of bilingualism were straightforward. The disease was diagnosed later in bilinguals than monolinguals, and in early-stage Alzheimer's disease bilinguals were coping with more disease pathology than monolinguals despite functioning at similar cognitive levels. It follows that bilinguals had more disease pathology for similar clinically observable levels of impairment, but the logic based on protection reverses in later stages of the disease. At some point, the greater degree of pathology that has accumulated in the bilingual brain will be impossible to overcome, and the decline in function will be more rapid than it is for monolinguals. The prediction, therefore, is that after some point of accumulated disease, cognitive decline will be more severe in bilingual patients than in monolinguals.

Like all research with Alzheimer's patients, carefully controlled experiments are difficult to execute. In advanced stages of the disease, fluctuations in cognitive alertness and the inability to complete most assessment instruments make standard research methods difficult to implement. Therefore, an indirect approach is required. Rather than directly study cognitive decline in advanced stages of the disease, our approach was to evaluate one aspect of decline in the earlier stages. The idea was that establishing differences in rate of decline at this point would at least suggest the post-diagnosis trajectory for bilingual patients in the longer term.

There are established rates at which an early form of cognitive decline, mild cognitive impairment (MCI), converts to Alzheimer's disease. These rates are set at around 10% to 15% annually [170]. There is not a simple straight line between the two conditions because there are varieties of mild cognitive impairment and not all of them are precursors to Alzheimer's disease, but on average, the linear relation between these cognitive disorders is clear. Therefore, the rate at which MCI converts to Alzheimer's disease should be different at different levels of cognitive reserve. To test this prediction, we identified monolingual and bilingual patients who were matched on important background variables and had been diagnosed with mild cognitive impairment. The study involved following them until the consensus definition by the team of medical experts in the clinic had changed from mild cognitive impairment to Alzheimer's disease. If the prediction is correct, then the conversion to Alzheimer's disease should be faster for bilinguals because they were older and had more advanced neuropathology when the symptoms of mild cognitive impairment were first detected. This is exactly what the results showed [171].

Not all conditions associated with neuropathology are as untreatable as Alzheimer's disease. One example is stroke, where an assault to the brain can cause damage to widespread cognitive and language systems. There are established rehabilitation protocols that are often able to restore some functioning despite permanent damage to the brain. Does bilingualism have any role in this recovery? In an interesting test of this possibility, Suvarna Alladi and colleagues [172] followed the cognitive recovery of monolingual and bilingual patients who had suffered strokes. All the patients were enrolled in intense therapeutic routines to help recover cognitive function. The dramatic finding was that twice as many bilingual patients (approximately 40%) recovered to normal cognitive levels that were comparable with their pre-stroke functioning than did monolingual patients (approximately 20%). Again, cognitive reserve may have boosted their cognitive resources and facilitated this recovery. Other studies have reported that bilinguals suffered less severe symptoms of stroke [173], multiple sclerosis, Parkinson's and Huntington's disease [174] than monolingual patients. These new studies tend to be small scale and preliminary —replication with larger samples is needed— but they raise the exciting possibility that cognitive reserve can have broader and more profound impact on cognitive health in older age than previously thought.

How much bilingualism and how soon?

The studies described so far have compared performance on some cognitive task or brain measure between groups of individuals who had spent most of their lives using mostly one language or multiple languages. These are rough comparisons and leave many questions about how much bilingual experience is necessary to achieve these outcomes. Current research in bilingualism now addresses this issue by looking for detailed relations between how much bilingual language use individuals have, what level of proficiency, what age bilingual language use began, what are the contexts in which they use the languages, and so on. All of these factors affect the type of outcome found for cognitive and brain measures, sometimes by showing that more bilingual experience is associated with larger outcomes and sometimes by showing that some threshold of bilingual experience is necessary for any outcomes. Bilingualism is complex, and each facet of the experience adds its own flavor. An important goal for future research is to document these pieces of bilingual experience and identify the role of each in the complex effects found in more general comparisons.

A different approach is to wind back to the beginning: does foreign language learning by monolingual older adults provide protection against cognitive decline? In other words, can language learning be used as an intervention for older adults to protect cognitive function? This idea has been discussed hypothetically by some researchers [175] but only a few studies have investigated the possibility experimentally. There is some preliminary evidence supporting the idea that older adults who were enrolled in language classes improved on some cognitive outcomes [176].

We recently took a different approach. We enrolled healthy monolingual older adults (around 70 years old) in a study, gave them all a set of background tests and specific tasks to measure executive functioning, and then divided them into three groups [177]. The first group was asked to spend 30 minutes per day for 16 weeks doing brain training exercises on a smartphone app. The second group spend the same amount of time using a language-learning app to learn Spanish. The third group was a control and did not engage in any training. After 16 weeks, the full set of executive functioning tasks was re-administered. The exercises on the brain-training app are similar to executive function tasks, so we expected individuals in that group to improve when we re-tested them at the end of the study. They did: scores on the tests at the end of the study were higher than they were in the first session. The control group did not do anything to change their ability with these tasks, and indeed, their scores at the end of the study were the same as they were at the beginning. But what about the Spanish group? Learning Spanish does not directly involve practicing executive functioning, but we expected there to be some improvement, possibly placing their performance between the other two groups. However, the results showed that the Spanish group improved almost as much as the brain training group on the tests. The only measure where the Spanish group did not improve as much was on speed. This is not surprising because the brain-training app required faster responses, but the Spanish app did not have time pressures. These results will potentially lead to new additions to the repertoire of interventions to help older adults to function at healthy cognitive levels, live independently, and enjoy life.

Bilingualism does not prevent Alzheimer's disease. Neither does it guarantee high levels of cognitive functioning and robust brains in older age. There is no magic bullet for any of these goals. But bilingualism is one factor that contributes to these outcomes and in the absence of effective pharmacological alternatives, this possibility is not trivial.

Take-away conclusions

- Cognitive reserve refers to a set of experiences that build resilience and allow cognitive levels to exceed the level expected by the state of the brain.
- Bilingualism contributes to cognitive reserve, so older bilinguals show cognitive function equivalent to that of monolinguals despite more brain atrophy for the bilinguals
- The greater resilience of bilingual brains extends to the early stages of dementia where bilinguals can function at healthy levels despite the accumulation of dementia pathology in the brain

Chapter 8
Why Bilingualism?

The languages we speak are essential to defining who we are. It is not a coincidence that colonizers throughout history have acted to replace local languages with the language of the empire, often with brutal consequences. The bilingual agenda is different: it seeks not to replace language but to accumulate languages, connecting individuals to their history and culture and creating a more nuanced composite identity and establish a more global world population with deeper and better means of connecting to each other. The consequences of such restructuring are profound.

The challenges, barriers, and opportunities offered by bilingualism are crystalized in the immigrant experience. For some immigrants, the old languages and old ways define their existence and cannot be easily abandoned. Many of these people who find it difficult to leave the old world behind may continue to live in the languages and traditions that have always defined them. But because they have relocated to a new environment, they may find that their children and grandchildren who have not learned this heritage language and these traditions may gradually slip away as the cultural and linguistic divide becomes greater. Language (and maybe food!) is the glue that keeps the generations together.

For others, the new life requires a new language and new attitudes, so the prospects associated with succeeding in that new life require embracing those languages and traditions. Immigrants who immerse themselves in the new language and culture may then raise their children as citizens of that adopted community. Should they also ensure that their progeny continue to speak the heritage language? Losing the home language is likely a greater risk for assimilated immigrants than for those who preserve the cultures and traditions; assimilated immigrants can communicate with their children in the new language. This short-term success may hasten the decay of the heritage language through the family lineage. The tension between adaptation and assimilation versus preservation and continuity is endemic to the immigrant experience. It is a profound problem that is not easily solved, but we can probably agree that the transmission of the heritage language is a worthy goal. And again —only half joking— this process might be fortified through the transmission of heritage foods. Eating is always easier than speaking, and food is steeped in culture!

Leaving behind one's past is not simple. Donia Clenman was a Holocaust survivor who immigrated to Canada after the war. She learned perfect English, married, and had children. Her children grew up to be completely Canadian, native speakers of English, and unburdened by a troubled European past. But the experience of immigration and assimilation always haunted her, as she describes in her poem, "I Dream in Good English Too" [178]:

> Sometimes
> I am a stranger to my family
> for I bring Europe's ghosts
> into the well-lit living room
> of Canadian internationalism –
> I was no child on arrival
> and yet, so well assimilated.
> Even my verses are native,
> and I dream in good English too.

Put this way, we can see that the most fundamental aspect of our human existence, our identity, is shaped by the languages we speak, and by the languages we do not speak. At the same time, the sociological structures and networks of our lives are also influenced by the language communities in which we participate. In a perspective that they call "socio-ecological", Nairan Ramirez-Esparza and colleagues trace the social structures associated with bilingualism to the structure of the worlds in which we engage [179]. Their argument is that we are shaped by our communities and our communities are determined by the languages and cultures with which we engage.

To this point, we have examined some of the ways in which being bilingual or learning a second language impacts language and cognitive concepts and abilities. But the influence of living with multiple languages may extend beyond these domains and impinge on more hidden, possibly more fundamental aspects of identity, potentially altering the way we exist in the world. The research exploring these possibilities is primarily conducted with adults, but since bilingual children typically grow up to become bilingual adults, insights from this work are central to understanding them.

Sociological and political dimensions of bilingualism

The political and sociological context of the community in which one lives has a substantial influence on the emergence and preservation of a bilingual populace. Bilingual communities require political will and social tolerance. At the center of these forces is the extent to which bilingualism is perceived as a positive or negative factor both for individuals and the community. Language policies have an important role in shaping those positions.

One measure of the extent to which a country tolerates or encourages bilingualism is the number of official languages it recognizes. Official language status is a legal term that identifies the language or languages that can be used in official government capacities. These are the languages in which individuals can expect to receive government services, including education, health care, official documentation and permits, and so on. The number varies widely: India has 23 official languages; Nigeria has one official language, English, along with more than 525 native languages; Switzerland has 4 official languages; Canada has 2 official languages. But how likely are citizens of those countries to be bilingual or multilingual? In other words, what is the relation between societal bilingualism and individual bilingualism? In the case of India and Nigeria, educated individuals are very likely to be multilingual; in the case of Switzerland and Canada, it is far less likely.

There is no simple connection between political declarations of official languages and individual or community adoption of multiple languages, especially if one considers only proficiency in the official languages. For example, the 2016 Canadian census indicated that only 17% of respondents stated they could conduct a conversation in both English and French, despite high levels of bilingualism in the country with heritage languages (over 60% in some urban centers). Similarly, Quebec, a Canadian province that is primarily French speaking, has enacted laws governing language use to protect French from being overrun by the English majority that surrounds it. These laws have successfully protected and advanced the use of French in Quebec but may also have had the effect of creating a French-speaking population that is more monolingual than it might otherwise have been. The political dimensions of language and bilingualism are real and present, but their consequences are not simple.

If official policy has such powerful effects on how languages are used in society, then why don't governments take the next step and pass laws supporting bilingualism? By the stroke of a pen, legislators could legitimize the disenfranchised speakers of minority languages, extend educational opportunity, and improve social cohesion and inclusivity. As described in Chapter 3, the United States tried several times to pass legislation guaranteeing access to minority language education through the Bilingual Education Act, a process that ended up involving the Supreme Court. But laws supporting bilingualism and bilingual education are difficult to pass, in part because of an underlying fear that bilingualism and bilingual education are actually harmful to children. The results is that policy makers, educators, and others are reluctant to take action [180]. The ancient fears that were implanted from the faulty intelligence testing research in the first half of the 20th century described in Chapter 5, remain influential. Motivated by different goals, the law governing the use of French in Quebec, Bill 101, was passed in 1977 and has been effective in expanding French language in the province but has come at considerable political cost throughout the country. Moreover, expanding French in Quebec has had negative impact on other languages, reducing their presence in public spaces in the community. Real change requires changes in policy and law, but these laws have consequences beyond the specific domains of language use.

Two languages, two personalities?

We know that languages differ not only in the words used to express meanings but also in the structures that are considered to be polite or acceptable. Speakers of some languages, such as Japanese or Hindi, are required to adjust the term used to address individuals to reflect the specific status relation with that person; speakers of other languages, such as English, would find that requirement baffling. Some years ago, a friend was teaching Japanese at a foreign university and shared a flat with other instructors in the Japanese department during the week, then traveled home for the weekend and non-teaching days. The arrangement was congenial; they were all glad to share the flat and all their communication was in Japanese. But things started to break down and life in the flat became tense. (Yes, it involved a boyfriend!) My friend knew that she had to speak to her flatmates, make the issue explicit, and come to a resolution. She also knew she could not do this in Japanese. The conversation would seem too direct, too confrontational, and Japanese simply did not have the vocabulary or structure to carry it out. So, for the first time, she addressed her flatmates and colleagues in English. She was the same person, and she knew that kind of direct speech was part of who she was, but she could not convey it in Japanese.

This example may illustrate what some researchers have described as greater social flexibility for bilinguals than monolinguals [179, 181]. Social flexibility allows bilinguals to engage in a greater range of social interactions by adapting to changing expectations and demands. Moreover, greater social flexibility has been associated with an increase in the quantity of social interactions, a less ethnocentric world view, and more acceptance of differences in others. In this sense, the bilingual individual may be more social, more open, and more tolerant than a monolingual individual. These attributes are part of personality profiles that vary across individuals. Does this mean that bilinguals have different personalities than monolinguals? Or more intriguingly, do bilinguals have different personalities when they are speaking in each of their languages?

There is evidence to suggest that at least the first of these possibilities is true. Bilinguals who have lived abroad score higher than those without that experience on tests measuring tolerance of ambiguity [182], a trait related to a wide range of positive behaviors in diverse social contexts. Moreover, bilingualism has also been associated with greater cognitive and cultural empathy, and open-mindedness: all presumably positive values to which we should aspire [183, 184].

Languages also embody different aspects of emotionality, so speakers of different languages have a different vocabulary and different range of emotional concepts they can convey. For this reason, forms of the emotional expressions available to bilinguals and the type of affect they can convey may be different from those for a monolingual speaker of that language [185]. More intriguingly, the experience of communicating through two different emotional linguistic systems may heighten emotional sensitivity overall, a skill essential for social interaction and empathy [186]. Nada Alqarni and Jean-Marc Dewaele [187] asked individuals who were Arabic-English bilinguals, Arabic monolinguals, or English monolinguals to identify emotional expressions in faces. Participants watched brief video clips of faces that were speaking in either English or Arabic and judged their emotional expression. For the conversations in English, the Arabic-English bilinguals were more accurate than the English monolinguals. For the conversations in Arabic, it was the Arabic monolinguals who were more accurate than the bilinguals. There are several possible reasons for this asymmetry. One is a simple design feature in that there was a much smaller sample size of Arabic monolinguals than there was for the other two groups. However, it is also possible that the results reflect differences between the languages (Arabic versus English) rather than differences between the speakers (monolingual versus bilingual). If different languages present a different pallet of emotional expressions, then bilingual speakers of those languages have access to the full range of experience and communication. The possibility of substantial differences in emotional sensitivity between monolingual and bilingual speakers is fascinating and requires further study.

Two languages, two modes of reasoning?

In the previous section we considered the possibility that bilinguals differ from monolinguals in affective or emotional reactivity, possibly because of structural or vocabulary differences between languages in how emotions are expressed. Could the same be true of cognitive reactivity? Is reasoning carried out differently across languages? And if so, does that mean that bilinguals arrive at different logical conclusions or make different decisions than monolinguals?

A dramatic example that supports this surprising possibility comes from research with the trolley problem. This thought scenario has a long history in the field of ethics. It has expanded over time to include many variations, but the essential issue is the same. The problem is presented as a scenario in which the listeners are asked to decide how they would act in a situation that is presented as a moral dilemma. In the standard scenario, a runaway trolley is heading along the track towards five people who are unable to move; all five will be killed when the trolley reaches them. There is a parallel track, and you (the listener) can intervene in the situation by pulling a lever to transfer the trolley to this other track. However, there is one person on that track who will be killed by the diverted trolley. What do you do? If you do nothing, five people will be killed, although you are not responsible; if you pull the lever, one person will be killed and you will be responsible, but the other five lives will be saved.

This is the basic structure of the problem, but many surface variations have been created. For example, instead of pulling a lever to divert the trolley, in some versions the listener is standing on a footbridge overlooking the track watching the events unfold. There is a large person (described in various levels of negative or derogatory detail) also on the bridge. The choice, therefore, is to push this person off the bridge to block the trolley and save the five lives, sacrificing this individual. In other variations, the certainty that the five people will be killed is adjusted to make it more probable than certain. The underlying moral structure of the question does not change, but one's emotional reaction to the problem is altered. It turns out that for all the variations of this problem and other similar situations involving life and death decisions, the decisions are made differently if the scenario is presented in your native language or in a second language, a difference called the "foreign language effect" [188]. A substantial body of research has now demonstrated that listeners are more likely to choose the option that deliberately sacrifices one person to save the other five when the problem is presented in a foreign language [189, 190]. This is called the utilitarian choice, because it prioritizes the greater good despite being based on an individual moral transgression.

The reason usually given for these results is that there is more emotional distance in a foreign language than in one's first or native language. This distance allows the individual to make the choice based on the rational and objective evaluation of one life versus five lives rather than the emotional bias in which the deliberate killing of one person is morally reprehensible. Aneta Pavlenko [191] also describes the increased emotional distance for speakers of a foreign language that enables them to utter words and sentences that they might find shocking in their native language. However, emotional distance alone does not fully explain the results.

In an interesting extension of the research, Michele Miozzo and colleagues [192] presented the trolley problem to bilinguals who were fully proficient in standard Italian and an Italian dialect, either Venetian or Bergamasque. All participants knew both languages from birth, and importantly, showed equivalent emotional attachment to both languages. There was no basis for the emotional distance argument. Yet, the effect replicated perfectly: more utilitarian choices were made when the problem was presented in the dialect than when it was presented in standard Italian. Therefore, the explanation for the foreign language effect in moral reasoning cannot be simply ascribed to emotional distance: other factors must be involved, although it is not clear at this time what those factors might be. The authors propose that the contexts in which the languages are used, as well as the relative informality of the dialect, may be relevant factors. They note as well that there are no written forms for the dialects, restricting their use to specific situations. The problem is intriguing and remains unsolved.

The foreign language effect is unsettling. We like to believe we are rational creatures guided by a moral code. How can we accept that we make different life and death decisions depending on the language in which the moral dilemma is presented? More troubling, we routinely allocate life and death decisions to elected officials, physicians, military and police personnel, and others. Should we be concerned that some of those decisions might have been different if the problem were presented in a different language? Of course, there is no answer, but what this body of research demonstrates is the profound role of language in our lives, not only in the obvious way in which it impacts cognition, but also in the hidden manners in which it may ultimately affect our lives.

Impacting the bottom line: Are there financial consequences of bilingualism?

As we just saw, important decisions appear to vary depending on the language in which the problem is presented. In the case of the trolley problem, one might argue that the decision that was made in the weaker language to sacrifice one person to save five lives was in some sense more "ethical". However, ethical is not an objective category in that it rises out of a set of circumstances that contribute to the judgment. Based on the trolley car problem alone, we would not want to conclude that bilinguals are simply more ethical than monolinguals!

Decisions about ethical behavior become particularly slippery when money is involved. We are all tempted by the prospect of increasing personal financial gain, and the decisions we make towards that end may sometimes cross into ethically grey territory. Are these ethical boundaries different for monolinguals and bilinguals? Or for bilinguals in their two languages? More broadly, some have suggested that cultural and ethnic factors have an impact on ethical business practices more generally [193].

Research on such large issues is difficult to conduct and precarious to generalize, but individual examples hint at the presence of larger patterns. In one such study, Pan and Patel [194] presented Chinese accounting students who were fluent in Chinese and English with an ethical accounting problem. Following the research with moral dilemmas like the trolley problem described above, they reasoned that similar influences might also shape decisions about accounting dilemmas. The participants were senior students who were about to enter the workforce and take up positions as accountants. Their English skills were excellent, and in fact their accounting program included some instruction through English.

As with all dilemmas, there are murky boundaries around the conditions for making a particular decision. In accounting, decisions are considered to be "aggressive" when they portray events more favorably than would be strictly indicated by the facts, moving such aggressive decisions towards territories that could be described as less ethical. The authors asked whether these Chinese students produced decisions that were more or less aggressive depending on the language in which the problem was presented. They argued that such accounting decisions might reflect cultural differences in the communities in which these languages are spoken: Chinese is associated with an interdependent mindset that is based on community needs, whereas English primes an independent mindset that is focused on the individual. These differences are also embedded in the languages: Chinese is inherently indirect and implicit, whereas English is largely direct and explicit. At a more social level, Chinese culture focuses more on interpersonal relationships, whereas English societies value personal attitudes and preferences. For these reasons, the authors predicted that the accounting students would be more likely to take actions to promote their own individual goals and express their unique needs when working in English than when they were given the same accounting problem in Chinese. This is exactly what they found: the participants made different decisions about reporting profits and losses when working in Chinese or English and used more aggressive accounting practices in English than in Chinese.

Most of us are not called upon to make accounting decisions, but the wealth we accumulate is an important feature of our lives. Because of the broad demographic situation in the U.S., there has been an incorrect inference that bilingualism is associated with lower socioeconomic status and lower wealth. The error reflects incorrect transitive reasoning: Most bilinguals in the U.S. are Hispanic, and most Hispanics in the U.S. live in relatively poor socioeconomic circumstances [195]. However, socioeconomic status is the result of many factors and has no implications for a relation between bilingualism and poverty. Is it possible to isolate a more direct relation between bilingualism and wealth?

We typically associate more skill and broader knowledge with enhanced opportunity and, as a consequence, a higher position. Logically, knowledge of other languages should constitute one such asset. Yet, in some places bilinguals often have worse jobs and make less money than their monolingual counterparts. How can we explain this counterintuitive finding? Patricia Gándara and colleagues [196, 197] argue that language is a form of "human capital", and as such, it enhances an individual's place in the labor market. However, other factors suppress or conceal that value, compromising the ability of bilinguals to achieve the status they might otherwise expect. Bilinguals are often immigrants and may have professional credentials that are not recognized in the new country, so their position in the social and economic hierarchy is compromised from the beginning. However, as Callahan and Gándara argue, when these factors are controlled, bilingualism provides a significant economic benefit.

In a clever approach, Gándara [197] turned the question upside down. Instead of asking what potential labor advantage might come from bilingualism, she asked whether the children of immigrants were *disadvantaged* when there was failure to support the development of their home language. Encouraging the development and maintenance of the heritage language is a simple way to produce bilingualism: little special effort, no formal classrooms, and no costly social programs are needed. Analyzing data from a long-term survey revealed clear patterns. The children of immigrants in this large sample who became functioning bilinguals by maintaining their heritage language earned higher salaries and had higher status occupations than did children of immigrants who became assimilated monolinguals and did not achieve proficiency in their heritage language. Even more compelling, the more bilingual these individuals were in terms of high proficiency in both languages, the better were these job market outcomes. It is logical that being bilingual should be an asset on the labor market, but because so many other factors are involved in these socioeconomic outcomes it is difficult to isolate the role of bilingual language proficiency. However, if one looks carefully, the evidence can be found.

A turning point in considering whether bilingualism is a handicap or an asset to children's development came from the Montreal study on children's intelligence by Peal and Lambert [106] described in Chapter 5. The researchers were aware that socioeconomic status was a complicating factor in all this research and had to be carefully controlled. Typically, research comparing monolingual and bilingual children examined monolingual children who spoke the majority community language and bilingual children who also spoke some minority heritage language. This situation tends to favor the majority language children for reasons beyond those related to their monolingual status; the typical example is English monolingual children in the U.S. and English-Spanish bilingual children. The innovation in the Peal and Lambert study was that all the children spoke French as their first language, a group for whom socioeconomic status was routinely lower than found for English-speaking children. Therefore, they reasoned that by comparing French-speaking children who were also fluent in English, the bilingual group, with their classmates who only spoke French, the monolingual group, they would be able to isolate the effect of bilingualism without contamination from socioeconomic status. Because French was the first language for all these children, the argument went, socioeconomic status was similar. The famous results from that study were that the bilingual children outperformed the monolinguals on all the tests.

Despite their best efforts, Peal and Lambert's assumption that they had ruled out socioeconomic status as a factor in these results was probably not correct. Even at that time, being bilingual improved job prospects and elevated socioeconomic status for both French and English speakers. In that sense, the monolingual and bilingual groups differed by more than just the number of languages they spoke. In the province of Quebec in 1970, the average annual salary for anglophone men was $8,171 Canadian dollars for monolinguals, and $8,938 for those who were bilingual because they also knew French, representing a "bilingual bonus" of just under 10%. In contrast, the average annual salary for francophone men was $5,136 for monolinguals and $7,363 for bilingual francophones, representing a bilingual bonus of just over 40% [198]. Francophones retained lower overall positions on socioeconomic status and received lower salaries than anglophones, but being bilingual nonetheless provided considerable upward mobility. Therefore, within the highly stratified social hierarchy of 1970s Quebec, there were large differences between anglophone and francophone communities in terms of wealth and prestige, but being able to speak both English and French improved social position in both language groups, with a greater benefit to the francophone community. The children in the Peal and Lambert study, therefore, also enjoyed greater social prestige and the advantages that accrued from that position.

Because language is so central to what we do and who we are, it should not be surprising that our language abilities —how many languages we know, as well as the relative status of those languages in the community— impact far more than just our capacity to communicate. As we have seen, there are effects on such disparate domains as emotional sensitivity, moral reasoning, and economic judgment and success that come both from the difference between speaking one versus two languages and from the specific languages involved. But these are complex effects that interact with many other factors: Bilingualism alone does not guarantee a good job or an empathic world view, yet it is one of the factors that contributes to those ends. These are presumably opportunities and values that we would wish to impart to our children, so, in that sense, they should also be considered in the development of bilingual children.

A last word

All our experiences leave a mark and, in some way, change who we are. An interest in music, a talent for painting, a predisposition for athletics, contribute to the choices we make, the skills we master, and the lives we lead. They also imprint themselves in our minds and brains. As we saw earlier, our brains adapt to the activities in which we regularly engage so they can carry them out more efficiently. The mind adapts to recurring activities by rewiring connections between networks of neurons, making those activities proceed somewhat differently for experts than for non-experts. Using language is arguably the most intense, extensive, and profound of all human activities. It would be astonishing if the way we used language had no consequence for our minds and brains.

We encounter languages in different ways, sometimes from home, sometimes from education, and sometimes from travel. These types of exposure to language are importantly different from each other. For children, the primary means of encountering and learning more than one language are through home heritage languages and bilingual education, or to a lesser extent, foreign language education. The central question we have examined in this book is how those language experiences, regardless of the means they are realized, impact children's development. And as we have seen over a wide variety of topics, the impact is inevitably complex, but also, it is invariably positive.

I have not said much about the process of learning a second language, either for children or for adults. In many ways, that is a different topic, although one I have addressed in the past [199]. Although more language proficiency is always better than less and often leads to larger effects of bilingualism, it is rarely decisive in determining whether bilingual language experience will impact cognition and development. Some people learn a second language more easily than others because they are more verbally talented or work harder at it, but the impact of bilingual language use is available to everyone, whatever proficiency level they achieve. Learning a language is always hard work, just as learning anything, musical performance or tennis, for example. I was recently at a conference where I met a hyperpolyglot who claimed to speak more than 30 languages. I had no reason to doubt him but neither did I have any means of verifying his claim! He described his process of language learning by explaining how he approached the most recent language he had added to his repertoire, Finnish. It was all a matter of hard work, practice, note keeping, practice, cross-checking, practice, and so on. There was no magic to it. But it is also true that anything that is hard for your brain is good for your brain, so just being engaged in the process of learning a language likely carries its own reward.

Parents spend much energy deliberating about language choices for their children. For some, the decision involves trying to figure out which languages to use in the home if parents are speakers of other languages, or which ones to use for specific types of conversations or activities. For others, the decision involves how to organize language education for their children either within school or as an addition to schooling. Parents have many questions and concerns about the potential impact of their decision on their children's development. But in all the head-scratching and deliberations that go on as they try to decide whether their children should become bilingual, there is one consequence of bilingualism that is almost never mentioned: *bilingual people can speak other languages!* They can read different books, travel to new places, communicate with other individuals, hold specialized jobs, study certain fields, and experience the world from a perspective not available to monolinguals. This alone should justify the journey.

Take-away conclusions

- The languages we speak have an impact beyond language and cognitive ability as there are effects found for reasoning and emotional decision making
- Being multilingual presents opportunities that may not be available to monolinguals, such as job choices and financial advancement
- Language is good; more language is better!

Epilogue
What do we Know?
Questions, Facts, and Myths

Research on bilingualism and its consequences has exploded in recent years. Not all of this research has focused on children, but all of it has added to our knowledge of bilingualism: how to define it, what it does (and does not) impact, and what decisions regarding bilingualism are in children's best interests. The answers to many of these questions are scattered throughout this book, so this epilogue distills some of that information around the questions that parents might find to be most pressing.

> 1. *Bilingual children often mix their languages and use the wrong one with the current speakers. Doesn't that mean they are confused?*

Adult bilinguals rarely make errors by inserting a word from the other language when it is not appropriate, but children do this frequently. However, they are not confused; they are making the most out of their resources. Since bilingual children know fewer words in each language than monolingual speakers of that language, they cleverly extend their resources to enhance communication by dipping into the other language. Bilingual children can distinguish between the languages from infancy, so there is no problem in understanding that they are separate. Their primary goal is to communicate. (Discussion in Chapter 1)

> 2. *But does the confusion show up in intelligence? Maybe bilingual children are "less intelligent" than monolingual children because they have too much to deal with from two languages.*

The early view that bilingualism causes mental confusion has been thoroughly discredited. For some measures, such as vocabulary knowledge in one language, monolingual children score higher than bilingual children; for some skills, such as attention and executive functioning, bilingual children perform better than monolingual children; and for other abilities, such as general nonverbal intelligence, reasoning, and planning, there are no differences between monolingual and bilingual children. The effects of bilingualism on children's development are specific, and there is no general deficit traceable to bilingual experience. (Discussion in Chapter 5)

3. *What is the best age to learn a new language? Can you master a new language after childhood?*

There is no doubt that children appear to have an easier time learning a new language than adults and that languages we learn at younger ages seem to be learned to a higher degree of proficiency than those we attempt to learn later. However, that is not the same as saying that there is a specific time window during which language learning is privileged. The idea that languages need to be learned in childhood to be properly mastered is the notion of a critical period. There are critical periods that control language learning, but they apply to learning a first language, not to adding a second language. A language can be learned at any time, but it is also true that the outcomes are typically better for languages learned in childhood. (Discussion in Chapter 2)

4. *Is it necessary to be bilingual from a young age to experience the cognitive and health-related benefits of bilingualism?*

Bilingualism is not an all-or-none experience – it is a continuum of experiences. Many of the effects of bilingualism found for cognitive outcomes and, to a lesser extent, health outcomes, have also been shown to be related to the *degree* of bilingual experience. Being more bilingual, being bilingual for a longer time, or simply using both languages more frequently are all associated with greater benefit to these outcomes. In this sense, bilingualism is no different from other experiences such as musical performance: the more you practice, the better you will play, and the more change can be expected to the neural pathways that guide that performance. (Discussion in Chapter 1)

5. *If two languages are good, are three languages even better?*

This question is hard to answer and there is no clear evidence either way. Some research studies comparing bilingual and multilingual individuals have found some additional benefits for trilinguals or multilinguals over bilinguals, but other studies investigating essentially the same question have found no extra advantage. One problem with these studies is that people who go on to become multilingual may differ from bilinguals in more ways than just the number of languages they speak. For example, they may be verbally gifted, more interested in languages, more educated, or other factors that could interfere with the outcome. In conducting research in which two groups are compared, it is essential that the groups differ only in the factor of interest; otherwise, no conclusions can be made. (Discussion in Chapter 5)

6. *Some children have special challenges that make school difficult and compromise academic achievement even in one language. Should they become bilingual? Should they be enrolled in bilingual education programs?*

There is no single answer to this question because there is no single reason that children have for learning a second language. For those with a learning disability who need to learn a heritage language at home, there is no evidence that adding on this language will further compromise that disability. In that case, the benefits of knowing the language and connecting to their family and community outweigh any additional effort that learning that language might bring. Parents considering bilingual education as an enrichment might find that a language program is not the best educational option for their child. The answer to the question, therefore, depends on the circumstances and reasons for the child's bilingual experience and the personal judgment of the parents regarding optimal educational choices. (Discussion in Chapter 3)

7. *There are several languages in our family, and we want our children to learn all of them. What language should we speak to them?*

Once we accept that listening to multiple languages does not confuse children, the problem of what to speak at home becomes easier to solve. The primary consideration is making communication as smooth and as meaningful as possible so there are no barriers to natural conversations in the family. The second consideration is making language a central part of family life: the more languages children hear, the more languages they learn. Parents also wonder if they should speak a language to their children in which they are not highly proficient or have a marked accent. There is no harm in this, but communication works best if everyone speaks the language in which they are most comfortable. (Discussion in Chapter 1)

8. *My child was diagnosed with dyslexia. Should she learn to read in a second language?*

Dyslexia is a generalized condition that impacts children's ability to learn to read and is caused by both genetic and environmental factors. For these children, reading is a struggle, but it is not a greater struggle to read in two languages. Bilingualism or biliteracy will not make the dyslexia go away, but it will not make it worse either. In this case, parents need to monitor the child's emotional response so that reading does not become too much of a burden or make the child too anxious. Reading will by definition be more difficult for a child with dyslexia; the child's overall well-being must guide these decisions. (Discussion in Chapter 4)

References

1. Harari, Y.N., *Sapiens: A brief history of humandkind*. 2015, New York: Harper.
2. Diamond, J., *The benefits of multilingualism*. Science, 2010. **330**: p. 332-333.
3. Grosjean, F., *Bilingual: Life and reality*. 2010, Cambridge, MA: Harvard University Press.
4. Byers-Heinlein, K., T.C. Burns, and J.F. Werker, *The roots of bilingualism in newborns*. Psychological Science, 2010. **21**: p. 343-348.
5. Nelson, C.A., N.A. Fox, and C.H. Zeanah, *Romania's Abandoned Children: Deprivation, Brain Development, and the Struggle for Recovery*. 2014, Cambridge, MA: Harvard University Press.
6. Saffran, J.R., A. Senghas, and J.C. Trueswell, *The acquisition of language by children*. Proceedings of the National Academy of Sciences, 2001. **98**(23): p. 12874–12875.
7. Richland, L.E., R.G. Morrison, and K.J. Holyoak, *Children's development of analogical reasoning: insights from scene analogy problems*. Journal of Experimental Child Psychology, 2006. **94**(3): p. 249-73.
8. Thomas, R.C. and L. Hasher, *Reflections of distraction in memory: Transfer of previous distraction improves recall in younger and older adults*. Journal of Experimental Psychology: Learning, Memory, and Cognition, 2012. **38**(1): p. 30-39.
9. Parsons, T.D., et al., *Sex differences in mental rotation and spatial rotation in a virtual environment*. Neuropsychologia, 2004. **42**(4): p. 555-62.
10. Boh, B., et al., *Processing of complex auditory patterns in musicians and nonmusicians*. PLoS One, 2011. **6**(7): p. e21458.
11. Bak, T.H., *Cooking pasta in La Paz*. Linguistic Approaches to Bilingualism, 2016. **6**: p. 699-717.
12. Bialystok, E., *The signal and the noise*. Linguistic Approaches to Bilingualism, 2016. **6**(5): p. 517-534.
13. Nichols, E.S., et al., *Bilingualism affords no general cognitive advantages: A population study of executive function in 11,000 people*. Psychological Science, 2020. **31**: p. 548-567.

14. Yamasaki, B.L. and G. Luk, *Eligibility for Special Education in Elementary School: The Role of Diverse Language Experiences.* Language, Speech, and Hearing Services in Schools, 2018. **49**(4): p. 889-901.

15. Luk, G. and J.F. Kroll, *Bilingualism and Education*, in *The Cambridge Handbook of Cognition and Education.* 2019. p. 292-319.

16. Green, D.W. and J. Abutalebi, *Language control in bilinguals: The adaptive control hypothesis.* Journal of Cognitive Psychology, 2013. **25**: p. 515-530.

17. Ronjat, J., *Le développement du langage observé chez un enfant bilingue.* 1913, Paris: Librairie Ancienne H. Champion.

18. Dopke, S., *One parent, one language: An interactional approach.* 1992, Amsterdam: John Benjamins.

19. De Houwer, A., *Parental language input patterns and children's bilingual use.* Applied Psycholinguistics, 2007. **28**: p. 411-424.

20. Saer, D.J., *The effects of bilingualism on intelligence.* British Journal of Psychology, 1923. **14**: p. 25-38.

21. Fernald, A., V.A. Marchman, and A. Weisleder, *SES differences in language processing skill and vocabulary are evident at 18 months.* Developmental Science, 2013. **16**(2): p. 234-248.

22. Hoff, E., *Interpreting the early language trajectories of children from low-SES and language minority homes: Implications for closing achievement gaps.* Developmental Psychology, 2013. **49**(1): p. 4-14.

23. Hart, B. and T.R. Risley, *Meaningful differences in the everyday experience of young American children.* 1995, Baltimore, MD: Brookes.

24. Sperry, D.E., L.L. Sperry, and P.J. Miller, *Reexamining the Verbal Environments of Children From Different Socioeconomic Backgrounds.* Child Development, 2019. **90**(4): p. 1303-1318.

25. Peets, K. and E. Bialystok, *Dissociating standardized and conversational measures of language proficiency in bilingual kindergarteners.* Applied Psycholinguistics, 2015. **36**: p. 437-461.

26. De Houwer, A., *Bilingual development in childhood.* Elements in Child Development. 2021, Cambridge: Cambridge University Press.

27. Byers-Heinlein, K., E. Morin-Lessard, and C. Lew-Williams, *Bilingual infants control their languages as they listen.*

Proceedings of the National Academy of Sciences, 2017. **114**: p. 9032-9037.

28.   Weikum, W.M., et al., *Visual language discrimination in infancy.* Science, 2007. **316**: p. 1159.

29.   Cuaya, L.V., et al., *Speech naturalness detection and language representation in the dog brain.* Neuroimage, 2021: p. 118811.

30.   Kroll, J.F., S.C. Bobb, and N. Hoshino, *Two languages in mind: Bilingualism as a tool to investigate language, cognition, and the brain.* Current Directions in Psychological Science, 2014. **23**: p. 159-163.

31.   Kandhadai, P., D.K. Danielson, and J.F. Werker, *Culture as a binder for bilingual acquisition.* Trends in Neuroscience and Education, 2014. **3**: p. 24-27.

32.   Lorenz, K., *King Solomon's Ring: New Light on Animal Ways.* 1952, New York: Crowell.

33.   Lewis, T.L. and D. Maurer, *Multiple sensitive periods in human visual development: evidence from visually deprived children.* Developmental Psychobiology, 2005. **46**(3): p. 163-83.

34.   Curtiss, S., *Genie: A psycholinguistic study of a modern-day "wild child".* 1977, New York: Academic Press.

35.   Mayberry, R.I. and R. Kluender, *Rethinking the critical period for language: New insights into an old question from American Sign Language.* Bilingualism: Language and Cognition, 2018. **21**(5): p. 886-905.

36.   Newport, E.L., *Maturational constraints on language learning.* Cognitive Science, 1990. **14**: p. 11-28.

37.   Werker, J.F. and T.K. Hensch, *Critical periods in speech perception: New directions.* Annual Review of Psychology, 2015. **66**: p. 173-196.

38.   Lenneberg, E.H., *Biological foundations of language.* 1967, New York: John Wiley.

39.   Bialystok, E. and J.F. Kroll, *The neurobiology of language: Looking beyond monolinguals.* Biolinguistics, 2017. **11**: p. 339-351.

40.   Krashen, S., *The critical period for language acquisition and its possible bases.* Annals of the New York Academy of Sciences, 1974. **263**: p. 211-224.

41.   Pinker, S., *The language instinct.* 1994, New York: W. Morrow.

42.   Johnson, J.S. and E.L. Newport, *Critical period effects in second language learning: The influence of maturational state on*

the acquisition of English as a second language. Cognitive Psychology, 1989. **21**: p. 60-99.

43. Hartshorne, J.K., J.B. Tenenbaum, and S. Pinker, *A critical period for second language acquisition: Evidence from 2/3 million English speakers.* Cognition, 2018. **177**: p. 263-277.

44. Birdsong, D., *The Critical Period Hypothesis for second language acquisition: Tailoring the coat of many colors,* in *Essential topics in applied linguistics and multilingualism,* M. Pawlak and D. Singleton, Editors. 2014, Springer International Publishing. p. 43-50.

45. Hakuta, K., E. Bialystok, and E. Wiley, *Critical evidence: A test of the critical-period hypothesis for second-language acquisition.* Psychological Science, 2003. **14**(1): p. 31-38.

46. DeLuca, V., et al., *Brain adaptations and neurological indices of processing in adult Second Language Acquisition: Challenges for the Critical Period Hypothesis* in *The Handbook of the Neuroscience of Multilingualism,* J. Schwieter, Editor. 2019, WileyBlackwell

47. Snow, C.E. and M. Hoefnagel-Hohle, *The Critical Period for Language Acquisition: Evidence from Second Language Learning.* Child Development, 1978. **49**: p. 114-1128.

48. Slik, F., et al., *Critical Period Claim Revisited: Reanalysis of Hartshorne, Tenenbaum, and Pinker (2018) Suggests Steady Decline and Learner-Type Differences.* Language Learning, 2021.

49. Krugman, P., *Arguing with Zombies: Economics, Politics, and the Fight for a Better Future.* 2020, New York: W.W. Norton.

50. Offord, D., V. Rjeoutski, and G. Argent, *The French Language in Russia: A Social, Political, Cultural, and Literary History.* 2018, Amsterdam: Amsterdam University Press.

51. Garcia, O. and H.H. Woodley, *Bilingual Education,* in *The Routledge Handbook of Educational Lingusitics,* M. Bigelow and J. Ennser-Kananen, Editors. 2015, Routledge: New York. p. 132-144.

52. Ovando, C.J., *Bilingual Education in the United States: Historical Development and Current Issues.* Bilingual Education in the United States, 2003. **27**: p. 1-24.

53. Nieto, D., *A brief history of bilingual education in the United States.* Perspectives on Urban Education, 2009. **6**: p. 61-72.

54. Pace, A., et al., *Measuring success: Within and cross-domain predictors of academic and social trajectories in elementary school.* Early Childhood Research Quarterly, 2019. **46**: p. 112-125.

55.   Democracy, F.f.E.a., *Democracy at risk: The need for a new federal policy in education.* 2008, The Forum for Education and Democracy: Washington, DC.

56.   Gándara, P., *Charting the relationship of the ESEA and English learners: One step forward, two steps back.* Russell Sage Foundation Journal of Social Sciences, 2015. **12**: p. 112-128.

57.   Lindholm-Leary, K. and N. Block, *Achievement in predominantly low SES/Hispanic dual language schools.* International Journal of Bilingual Education and Bilingualism, 2010. **13**(1): p. 43-60.

58.   Lindholm-Leary, K., *Bilingual and biliteracy skills in young Spanish-speaking low-SES children: impact of instructional language and primary language proficiency.* International Journal of Bilingual Education and Bilingualism, 2014. **17**(2): p. 144-159.

59.   Thomas-Sunesson, D., K. Hakuta, and E. Bialystok, *Degree of bilingualism modifies executive control in Hispanic children in the USA.* International Journal of Bilingual Education and Bilingualism, 2018. **21**: p. 197-206.

60.   Barik, H.C. and M. Swain, *Three Year Evaluation of Large-Scale Early Grade French Immersion Program: The Ottawa Study.* Language Learning, 1975. **25**(1): p. 1-30.

61.   Genesee, F., *What do we know about bilingual education for majority language students,* in *Handbook of Bilingualism and Multiculturalism*, T.K. Bhatia and W. Ritchie, Editors. 2004, Blackwell: Malden, MA. p. 547-576.

62.   Hermanto, N., S. Moreno, and E. Bialystok, *Linguistic and metalinguistic outcomes of intense immersion education: How bilingual?* International Journal of Bilingual Education and Bilingualism, 2012. **15**(2): p. 131-145.

63.   Swain, M. and S. Lapkin, *Evaluating bilingual education: A Canadian case study.* 1982, Clevedon: Multilingual Matters.

64.   Bild, E.-R. and M. Swain, *Minority language students in a French immersion programme: Their French proficiency.* Journal of Multilingual and Multicultural Development, 1989. **10**: p. 255-274.

65.   Au-Yeung, K., et al., *Development of English and French Language and Literacy Skills in EL1 and EL French Immersion Students in the Early Grades.* Reading Research Quarterly, 2015. **50**: p. 233-254.

66. Shorbagi, S.H., C. Dias Martins, and E. Bialystok, *Acquiring the language of instruction: Effect of home language experience.* Applied Psycholinguistics, 2022. **43**: p. 463-484.
67. Montanari, S., *A case study of bi-literacy development among children enrolled in an Italian–English dual language program in Southern California.* International Journal of Bilingual Education and Bilingualism, 2013. **17**(5): p. 509-525.
68. Padilla, A.M., et al., *A Mandarin/English two-way immersion program: Language proficiency and academic achievement.* Foreign Language Annals, 2013. **46**(4): p. 661-679.
69. Schwartz, M., *The impact of the First Language First model on vocabulary development among preschool bilingual children.* Reading and Writing, 2013. **27**(4): p. 709-732.
70. Schwartz, M. and Y. Shaul, *Narrative development among language-minority children: the role of bilingual versus monolingual preschool education.* Language, Culture and Curriculum, 2013. **26**(1): p. 36-51.
71. Dunn, L.M. and D.M. Dunn, *Peabody Picture Vocabulary Test-Fourth Edition.* 2007, Bloomington, MN: NCS Pearson Inc.
72. Bialystok, E., et al., *Receptive vocabulary differences in monolingual and bilingual children.* Bilingualism: Language and Cognition, 2010. **13**(4): p. 525-531.
73. Leonard, L.B., *Children with Specific Language Impairment.* 2014, Cambridge, USA: MIT Press.
74. Kohnert, K., J. Windsor, and K.D. Ebert, *Primary or "specific" language impairment and children learning a second language.* Brain and Language, 2009. **109**(2-3): p. 101-11.
75. Paradis, J., *The interface between bilingual development and specific language impairment.* Applied Psycholinguistics, 2010. **31**(2): p. 227-252.
76. Bedore, L.M. and E.D. Peña, *Assessment of bilingual children for identification of Language Impairment: Current findings and implications for practice.* International Journal of Bilingual Education and Bilingualism, 2008. **11**(1): p. 1-29.
77. Peña, E.D., et al., *Identifying Developmental Language Disorder in School Age Bilinguals: Semantics, Grammar, and Narratives.* Language Assessment Quarterly, 2020. **17**(5): p. 541-558.
78. Pratt, A.S., et al., *Exploring the Use of Parent and Teacher Questionnaires to Screen for Language Disorders in Bilingual Children.* Topics in Early Childhood Special Education, 2020.

79. Kohnert, K., *Language disorders in bilingual children and adults. Second edition.* 2013, San Diego: Plural Publishing.
80. Afflerbach, P., ed. *Handbook of individual differences in reading: Reader, text, and context.* 2015, Routledge: New York.
81. Adams, M.J., *Beginning to read: Thinking and learning about print.* 1990, Cambridge, MA: MIT Press.
82. Castles, A., K. Rastle, and K. Nation, *Ending the Reading Wars: Reading Acquisition From Novice to Expert.* Psychological Science in the Public Interest, 2018. **19**(1): p. 5-51.
83. Hoover, W.A. and P.B. Gough, *The simple view of reading.* Reading and Writing: An Interdisciplinary Journal, 1990. **2**(2): p. 127-160.
84. Goldenberg, C., *Reading Wars, Reading Science, and English Learners.* Reading Research Quarterly, 2020. **55**(S1).
85. Umbel, V.M., et al., *Measuring Bilingual Children's Receptive Vocabularies.* Child Development, 1992. **63**(4): p. 1012-1020.
86. Gross, M., M. Buac, and M. Kaushanskaya, *Conceptual scoring of receptive and expressive vocabulary measures in simultaneous and sequential bilingual children.* American Journal of Speech and Language Pathology, 2014. **23**(4): p. 574-86.
87. Bialystok, E. and G. Luk, *Receptive vocabulary differences in monolingual and bilingual adults.* Bilingualism-Language and Cognition, 2012. **15**(2): p. 397-401.
88. Huang, B.H., et al., *The contributions of oral language to English reading outcomes among young bilingual students in the United States.* International Journal of Bilingualism, 2021. **25**(1): p. 40-57.
89. Bialystok, E., G. Luk, and E. Kwan, *Bilingualism, biliteracy, and learning to read: Interactions among languages and writing systems.* Scientific Studies of Reading, 2005. **9**(1): p. 43-61.
90. Cummins, J., *Bilingualism and the development of metalinguistic awareness.* Journal of Cross-Cultural Psychology, 1978. **9**: p. 131-149.
91. Galambos, S.J. and K. Hakuta, *Subject-specific and task-specific characteristics of metalinguistic awareness in bilingual children.* Applied Psycholinguistics, 1988. **9**: p. 141-162.
92. Bialystok, E., *Factors in the growth of linguistic awareness.* Child Development, 1986. **57**(2): p. 498-510.
93. Bialystok, E., *Symbolic representation across domains in preschool children.* Journal of Experimental Child Psychology, 2000. **76**(3): p. 173-189.

94. Cain, K., J. Oakhill, and P. Bryant, *Children's reading comprehension ability: Concurrent prediction by working memory, verbal ability, and component skills.* Journal of Educational Psychology, 2004. **96**(1): p. 31-42.

95. Geva, E. and L.S. Siegel, *Orthographic and cognitive factors in the concurrent development of basic reading skills in two languages.* Reading and Writing: An Interdisciplinary Journal, 2000. **12**: p. 1-30.

96. Morales, J., A. Calvo, and E. Bialystok, *Working memory development in monolingual and bilingual children.* Journal of Experimental Child Psychology, 2013. **114**(2): p. 187-202.

97. Greenberg, A., B. Bellana, and E. Bialystok, *Perspective-taking ability in bilingual children: Extending advantages in executive control to spatial reasoning.* Cognitive Development, 2013. **28**(1): p. 41-50.

98. Hsin, L. and C. Snow, *Social perspective taking: a benefit of bilingualism in academic writing.* Reading and Writing, 2017. **30**(6): p. 1193-1214.

99. Bruner, J.S., J.J. Goodnow, and G.A. Austin, *A study of thinking.* 1956, New York: Wiley.

100. Chomsky, N., *Aspects of the theory of syntax.* 1965, Cambridge MA: MIT Press.

101. Goodenough, F.L., *Racial differences in the intelligence of school children.* Journal of Experimental Psychology, 1926. **9**: p. 388-397.

102. Darcy, N.T., *The effect of bilingualism upon the measurement of the intelligence of children of preschool age.* Journal of Educational Psychology, 1946. **37**: p. 21-44.

103. Darcy, N.T., *A review of the literature on the effects of bilingualism upon the measurement of intelligence.* Journal of Genetic Psychology, 1953. **82**(1): p. 21-57.

104. Darcy, N.T., *Bilingualism and the measurement of intelligence: A review of a decade of research.* Journal of Genetic Psychology, 1963. **103**: p. 259-282.

105. Gould, S.J., *The mismeasure of man.* 1981, New York: Norton.

106. Peal, E. and W. Lambert, *The relation of bilingualism to intelligence.* Psychological Monographs, 1962. **76 (Whole No. 546)**: p. 1-23.

107. Bialystok, E., et al., *The swerve: How childhood bilingualism changed from liability to benefit.* Developmental Psychology, 2022.

108. Duncan, G.J., K.M. Ziol-Guest, and A. Kalil, *Early childhood poverty and adult attainment, behavior, and health.* Child Development, 2010. **81**: p. 306-325.

109. Mischel, W., Y. Shoda, and M.L. Rodriguez, *Delay of gratification in children.* Science, 1989. **244**: p. 933-938.

110. Barac, R., et al., *The cognitive development of young dual language learners: A critical review.* Early Childhood Research Quarterly, 2014. **29**: p. 699-714.

111. Schroeder, S.R., *Do Bilinguals Have an Advantage in Theory of Mind? A Meta-Analysis.* Frontiers in Communication, 2018. **3**.

112. Fan, S.P., et al., *The exposure advantage: Early exposure to a multilingual environment promotes effective communication.* Psychological Science 2015. **26**. p. 1090-1097.

113. Morton, J.P. and S.N. Harper, *What did Simon say? Revisiting the bilingual advantage.* Developmental Science, 2007. **10**: p. 719-726.

114. Hartanto, A., W.X. Toh, and H. Yang, *Bilingualism narrows socioeconomic disparities in executive functions and self-regulatory behaviors during early childhood: Evidence from the early childhood longitudinal study.* Child Development, 2019. **90**(4): p. 1215-1235.

115. Calvo, A. and E. Bialystok, *Independent effects of bilingualism and socioeconomic status on language ability and executive functioning.* Cognition, 2014. **130**(3): p. 278-88.

116. Krizman, J., E. Skoe, and N. Kraus, *Bilingual enhancements have no socioeconomic boundaries.* Developmental Science, 2016. **19**(6): p. 881-891.

117. Engel de Abreu, P.M., et al., *Bilingualism enriches the poor: Enhanced cognitive control in low-income minority children.* Psychological Science, 2012. **23**: p. 1364-1371.

118. Werker, J.F. and K. Byers-Heinlein, *Bilingualism in infancy: first steps in perception and comprehension.* TRENDS in Cognitive Sciences, 2008. **12**(4): p. 144-151.

119. Kovacs, A.M. and J. Mehler, *Cognitive gains in 7-month-old bilingual infants.* Proceedings of the National Academy of Science, 2009. **106**(16): p. 6556-60.

120. Comishen, K., E. Bialystok, and S.A. Adler, *The impact of bilingual environments on selective attention in infancy.* Developmental Science, 2019. **22**: p. e12797.

121. D'Souza, D., et al., *Is mere exposure enough? The effects of bilingual environments on infant cognitive development.* Royal Society Open Science, 2020. **7**: p. 180191.

122. Rauscher, F.H., G.L. Shaw, and K.N. Ky, *Music and spatial task performance.* Nature, 1993. **365**: p. 611.

123. Antoniou, M., *The advantages of bilingualism debate.* Annual Review of Linguistics, 2019. **5**: p. 1-21.

124. Bialystok, E., *Null results in bilingualism research: What they tell us and what they don't.* Journal of Multilingual Theories and Practices, 2020. **1**(1): p. 8-22.

125. Kousaie, S. and N.A. Phillips, *A behavioural and electrophysiological investigation of the effect of bilingualism on aging and cognitive control.* Neuropsychologia, 2017. **94**: p. 23-35.

126. Renier, L.A., et al., *Preserved functional specialization for spatial processing in the middle occipital gyrus of the early blind.* Neuron, 2010. **68**(1): p. 138-148.

127. Draganski, B., et al., *Changes in grey matter induced by training.* Nature, 2004. **427**: p. 311-312.

128. Mechelli, A., et al., *Structural plasticity in the bilingual brain.* Nature, 2004. **431**: p. 757.

129. Grundy, J.G., J.A.E. Anderson, and E. Bialystok, *Neural correlates of cognitive processing in monolinguals and bilinguals.* Annals of the New York Academy of Sciences, 2017. **1396**(1): p. 183-201.

130. DeLuca, V., et al., *Redefining bilingualism as a spectrum of experiences that differentially affects brain structure and function.* Proceedings of the National Academy of Sciences, 2019. **116**(15): p. 7565-7574.

131. Noble, K.G., et al., *Neural correlates of socioeconomic status in the developing human brain.* Developmental Science, 2012. **15**(4): p. 516-27.

132. Brito, N.H. and K.G. Noble, *The independent and interacting effects of socioeconomic status and dual-language use on brain structure and cognition.* Developmental Science, 2018: p. e12688.

133. Berken, J.A., et al., *The timing of language learning shapes brain structure associated with articulation.* Brain Structure and Function, 2016. **221**(7).

134. Mohades, S.G., et al., *DTI reveals structural differences in white matter tracts between bilingual and monolingual children.* Brain Research, 2012. **1435**: p. 72-80.

135. Mohades, S.G., et al., *White-Matter development is different in bilingual and monolingual children: A longitudinal DTI study.* PLoS One, 2015. **10**(2): p. e0117968.

136.   Pliatsikas, C., et al., *The effect of bilingualism on brain development from early childhood to young adulthood.* Brain Structure and Function, 2020. **225**(7): p. 2131-2152.

137.   Berken, J.A., V.L. Gracco, and D. Klein, *Early bilingualism, language attainment, and brain development.* Neuropsychologia, 2017. **98**: p. 220-227.

138.   Arredondo, M.M., et al., *Bilingual exposure enhances left IFG specialization for language in children.* Bilingualism: Language and Cognition, 2019. **22**(4): p. 783-801.

139.   Koen, J.D. and M.D. Rugg, *Neural Dedifferentiation in the Aging Brain.* Trends in Cognitive Sciences, 2019. **23**(7): p. 547-559.

140.   Bernardi, G., et al., *How skill expertise shapes the brain functional architecture: an fMRI study of visuo-spatial and motor processing in professional racing-car and naive drivers.* PLoS One, 2013. **8**(10): p. e77764.

141.   Kovelman, I., S.A. Baker, and L.A. Petitto, *Bilingual and monolingual brains compared: a functional magnetic resonance imaging investigation of syntactic processing and a possible "neural signature" of bilingualism.* Journal of Cognitive Neuroscience, 2008. **20**(1): p. 153-169.

142.   Arredondo, M.M., et al., *Bilingualism alters children's frontal lobe functioning for attentional control.* Developmental Science, 2017. **20**(3): p. e12377.

143.   Mercure, E., et al., *Language experience impacts brain activation for spoken and signed language in infancy: Insights from unimodal and bimodal bilinguals.* Neurobiology of Language, 2020. **1**(1): p. 9-32.

144.   Pierce, L.J., et al., *Mapping the unconscious maintenance of a lost first language.* Proceedings of the National Academy of Science, 2015. **112**(8): p. E922.

145.   Jasinska, K.K. and L.A. Petitto, *Development of neural systems for reading in the monolingual and bilingual brain: new insights from functional near infrared spectroscopy neuroimaging.* Developmental Neuropsychology, 2014. **39**(6): p. 421-39.

146.   Jasinska, K.K., et al., *Bilingualism yields language-specific plasticity in left hemisphere's circuitry for learning to read in young children.* Neuropsychologia, 2017. **98**: p. 34-45.

147.   Macnamara, J., *The effect of instruction in a weaker language.* Journal of Social Issues, 1967. **23**: p. 121-135.

148.   Mondt, K., et al., *Neural differences in bilingual children's arithmetic processing depending on language of instruction.* Mind, Brain, and Education, 2011. **5**(2): p. 79-88.

149. Cummings, J., et al., *Alzheimer's disease drug development pipeline: 2017.* Alzheimer's & Dementia: Translational Research & Clinical Interventions, 2017. **3**(3): p. 367-384.

150. Stern, Y., *What is cognitive reserve? Theory and research application of the reserve concept.* Journal of the International Neuropsychological Society, 2002. **8**: p. 448-460.

151. Bialystok, E., J.A.E. Anderson, and J.G. Grundy, *Interpreting cognitive decline in the face of cognitive reserve: Does bilingualism affect cognitive aging?* Linguistic Approaches to Bilingualism, 2021. **11**(4): p. 484-504.

152. Abutalebi, J., et al., *Bilingualism provides a neural reserve for aging populations.* Neuropsychologia, 2015. **69**: p. 201-10.

153. Abutalebi, J., et al., *Bilingualism protects anterior temporal lobe integrity in aging.* Neurobiology of Aging, 2014. **35**(9): p. 2126-33.

154. Abutalebi, J., et al., *The neuroprotective effects of bilingualism upon the inferior parietal lobule: A structural neuroimaging study in aging Chinese bilinguals.* Journal of Neurolinguistics, 2015. **33**: p. 3-13.

155. Olsen, R.K., et al., *The effect of lifelong bilingualism on regional grey and white matter volume.* Brain Research, 2015. **1612**: p. 128-39.

156. Gold, B.T., N.F. Johnson, and D.K. Powell, *Lifelong bilingualism contributes to cognitive reserve against white matter integrity declines in aging.* Neuropsychologia, 2013. **51**(13): p. 2841-2846.

157. Anderson, J.A.E., et al., *Bilingualism contributes to reserve and working memory efficiency: Evidence from structural and functional neuroimaging.* Neuropsychologia, 2021. **163**: p. 108071.

158. Del Maschio, N., et al., *Neuroplasticity across the lifespan and aging effects in bilinguals and monolinguals.* Brain and Cognition, 2018. **125**: p. 118-126.

159. Heim, S., et al., *Bilingualism and "Brain Reserve": A matter of age.* Neurobiology of Aging, 2019. **81**: p. 157-165.

160. Berkes, M., et al., *Poorer clinical outcomes for older adult monolinguals when matched to bilinguals on brain health.* Brain Structure and Function, 2021. **226**: p. 415-424.

161. Bialystok, E., F.I.M. Craik, and M. Freedman, *Bilingualism as a protection against the onset of symptoms of dementia.* Neuropsychologia, 2007. **45**(2): p. 459-464.

162. Anderson, J.A.E., K. Hawrylewicz, and J.G. Grundy, *Does bilingualism protect against dementia? A meta-analysis.* Psychonomic Bulletin & Review, 2020. **27**(5): p. 952-965.

163. Paulavicius, A.M., et al., *Bilingualism for delaying the onset of Alzheimer's disease: a systematic review and meta-analysis.* European Geriatric Medicine, 2020.

164. Schweizer, T.A., et al., *Bilingualism as a contributor to cognitive reserve: Evidence from brain atrophy in Alzheimer's disease.* Cortex, 2012. **48**(8): p. 991-996.

165. Kowoll, M.E., et al., *Bilingualism as a contributor to cognitive reserve? Evidence from cerebral glucose metabolism in Mild Cognitive Impairment and Alzheimer's Disease.* Frontiers in Psychiatry, 2016. **7**.

166. Perani, D., et al., *The impact of bilingualism on brain reserve and metabolic connectivity in Alzheimer's dementia.* Proceedings of the National Academy of Sciences, 2017: p. 201610909.

167. Brookmeyer, R., et al., *Forecasting the global burden of Alzheimer's disease.* Alzheimers & Dementia, 2007. **3**(3): p. 186-91.

168. Klein, R.M., J. Christie, and M. Parkvall, *Does multilingualism affect the incidence of Alzheimer's disease?: A worldwide analysis by country.* SSM - Population Health, 2016. **2**: p. 463-467.

169. Bialystok, E., et al., *Effects of bilingualism on the age of onset and progression of MCI and AD: evidence from executive function tests.* Neuropsychology, 2014. **28**(2): p. 290-304.

170. Petersen, R.C., et al., *Current concepts in Mild Cognitive Impairment.* Archives of Neurology, 2001. **58**: p. 1985-1992.

171. Berkes, M., et al., *Conversion of Mild Cognitive Impairment to Alzheimer Disease in Monolingual and Bilingual Patients.* Alzheimer's Disease and Associated Disorders, 2020. **34**: p. 225-230.

172. Alladi, S., et al., *Impact of bilingualism on cognitive outcome after stroke.* Stroke, 2016. **47**: p. 258-261.

173. Paplikar, A., et al., *Bilingualism and the severity of poststroke aphasia.* Aphasiology, 2019. **33**(1): p. 58-72.

174. Voits, T., et al., *Beyond Alzheimer's disease: Can bilingualism be a more generalized protective factor in neurodegeneration?* Neuropsychologia, 2020. **147**: p. 107593.

175. Antoniou, M., G.M. Gunasekera, and P.C. Wong, *Foreign language training as cognitive therapy for age-related cognitive decline: a hypothesis for future research.* Neuroscience and Biobehavioral Reviews, 2013. **37**: p. 2689-2698.

176. Wong, P.C.M., et al., *Language training leads to global cognitive improvement in older adults: A preliminary study.* Journal of Speech, Language, and Hearing Research, 2019. **62**(7): p. 2411-2424.
177. Meltzer, J.A., et al., *Improvement in executive function for older adults through smartphone apps: a randomized clinical trial comparing language learning and brain training.* Aging, Neuropsychology, and Cognition, 2021: p. 1-22.
178. Clenman, D.B., *I Dream in Good English Too.* 1988, Toronto: Flowerfield and Littleman.
179. Ramirez-Esparza, N., A. Garcia-Sierra, and S. Jiang, *The current standing of bilingualism in today's globalized world: a socio-ecological perspective.* Current Opinion in Psychology, 2020. **32**: p. 124-128.
180. Kroll, J.F. and P.E. Dussias, *The Benefits of multilingualism to the personal and professional development of residents of the US.* Foreign Language Annals, 2017. **50**(2): p. 248-259.
181. Ikizer, E.G. and N. Ramirez-Esparza, *Bilinguals' social flexibility.* Bilingualism: Language and Cognition, 2018. **21**(5): p. 957-969.
182. Dewaele, J.-M. and L. Wei, *Is multilingualism linked to a higher tolerance of ambiguity?* Bilingualism: Language and Cognition, 2013. **16**: p. 231-240.
183. Dewaele, J.-M. and L. Wei, *Multilingualism, empathy and multicompetence.* International Journal of Multilingualism, 2012. **9**: p. 352-366.
184. Dewaele, J.-M. and E. Botes, *Does multilingualism shape personality? An exploratory investigation.* International Journal of Bilingualism, 2019.
185. Pavlenko, A., *Emotion and emotion-laden words in the bilingual lexicon.* Bilingualism: Language and Cognition, 2008. **11**(2): p. 147-164.
186. Pavlenko, A., *Emotions and multilingualism.* 2005, Cambridge, MA: Cambridge University press.
187. Alqarni, N. and J.-M. Dewaele, *A bilingual emotional advantage? An investigation into the effects of psychological factors in emotion perception in Arabic and in English of Arabic-English bilinguals and Arabic/English monolinguals.* International Journal of Bilingualism, 2020. **24**: p. 141-158.
188. Keysar, B., S.L. Hayakawa, and S.G. An, *The foreign-language effect: thinking in a foreign tongue reduces decision biases.* Psychological Science, 2012. **23**(6): p. 661-8.

189.   Costa, A., M.L. Vives, and J.D. Corey, *On language processing shaping decision making.* Current Directions in Psychological Science, 2017. **26**(2): p. 146-151.

190.   Hayakawa, S., et al., *Using a foreign language changes our choices.* Trends in Cognitive Sciences, 2016. **20**(11): p. 792-793.

191.   Pavlenko, A., *Affective processing in bilingual speakers: disembodied cognition?* International Journal of Psychology, 2012. **47**(6): p. 405-28.

192.   Miozzo, M., et al., *Foreign language effect in decision-making: How foreign is it?* Cognition, 2020. **199**: p. 104245.

193.   McDonald, G., *Cross-cultural methodological issues in ethical research.* Journal of Business Ethics, 2000. **27**: p. 89-104.

194.   Pan, P. and C. Patel, *The Influence of Native Versus Foreign Language on Chinese Subjects' Aggressive Financial Reporting Judgments.* Journal of Business Ethics, 2018. **150**(3): p. 863-878.

195.   Noe-Bustmante, L. and A. Flores, *Facts on Latinos in the U.S.* 2019, Pew Research Center.

196.   Callahan, R.M. and P.C. Gándara, *The bilingual advantage: Language, literacy, and the US labor market.* 2014: Multilingual Matters.

197.   Gándara, P., *The economic value of bilingualism in the United States.* Bilingual Research Journal, 2018. **41**(4): p. 334-343.

198.   Vaillancourt, F., D. Lemay, and L. Vaillancourt, *Laggards no more: The changed socioeconomic status of francophones in Quebec.* 2007, C.D. Howe Institute Backgrounder.

199.   Bialystok, E. and K. Hakuta, *In other words: The psychology and science of second language acquisition.* 1994, New York: Basic Books.

About the Author

Dr. Ellen Bialystok, OC, PhD, FRSC

Ellen Bialystok is a Distinguished Research Professor of Psychology and Associate Scientist at the Rotman Research Institute of the Baycrest Centre for Geriatric Care. She is an Officer of the Order of Canada and a Fellow of the Royal Society of Canada.

Her research uses behavioral and neuroimaging methods to examine the effect of bilingualism on cognitive processes across the lifespan. Her discoveries include the identification of differences in the development of essential cognitive and language abilities for bilingual children, the use of different brain networks by monolingual and bilingual young adults performing simple conflict tasks, and the postponement of symptoms of dementia in bilingual older adults.

Among her awards are the Canadian Society for Brain Behaviour and Cognitive Science Hebb Award (2011), Killam Prize for the Social Sciences (2010), York University President's Research Award of Merit (2009), Donald T. Stuss Award for Research Excellence at the Baycrest Geriatric Centre (2005), Dean's Award for Outstanding Research (2002), Killam Research Fellowship (2001), and the Walter Gordon Research Fellowship (1999). In 2017 she was granted an honorary doctorate from the University of Oslo for her contributions to research.

TBR BOOKS

a program of CALEC

About TBR Books

TBR Books is a program of the Center for the Advancement of Languages, Education, and Communities. We publish researchers and practitioners who seek to engage diverse communities on topics related to education, languages, cultural history, and social initiatives. We translate our books in a variety of languages to further expand our impact.

BOOKS IN ENGLISH

The Heart of an Artichoke by Linda Ashour and Claire Lerognon

French All Around us by Kathleen Stein-Smith and Fabrice Jaumont

Navigating Dual Immersion: A Teacher's Companion for the School Year and Beyond by Valerie Sun

Conversations on Bilingualism by Fabrice Jaumont

One Good Question: How to Ask Challenging Questions that Lead You to Real Solutions by Rhonda Broussard

Bilingual Children: Families, Education, and Development by Ellen Bialystok

Can We Agree to Disagree? by Sabine Landolt and Agathe Laurent

Salsa Dancing in Gym Shoes by Tammy Oberg de la Garza and Alyson Leah Lavigne

Beyond Gibraltar; The Other Shore; Mamma in her Village by Maristella de Panizza Lorch

The Clarks of Willsborough Point by Darcey Hale

The English Patchwork by Pedro Tozzi and Giovanna de Lima

Peshtigo 1871 by Charles Mercier

The Word of the Month by Ben Lévy, Jim Sheppard, Andrew Arnon

Two Centuries of French Education in New York: The Role of Schools in Cultural Diplomacy by Jane Flatau Ross

The Bilingual Revolution: The Future of Education is in Two Languages by Fabrice Jaumont

BOOKS IN OTHER LANGUAGES

Deux siècles d'enseignement français à New York : le rôle des écoles dans la diplomatie culturelle by Jane Flatau Ross

Sénégalais de l'étranger by Maya Smith

Le projet Colibri : créer à partir de "rien" by Vickie Frémont

Pareils mais différents by Sabine Landolt and Agathe Laurent

Le don des langues by Kathleen Stein-Smith and Fabrice Jaumont

BOOKS FOR CHILDREN (available in several languages)

Franglais Soup e by Adrienne Mei

Rainbows, Masks, and Ice Cream by Deana Sobel Lederman

Korean Super New Years with Grandma by Mary Chi-Whi Kim and Eunjoo Feaster

Math for All by Mark Hansen

Rose Alone by Sheila Decosse

Uncle Steve's Country Home; The Blue Dress; The Good, the Ugly, and the Great by Teboho Moja

Immunity Fun!; Respiratory Fun!; Digestive Fun! By Dounia Stewart-McMeel

Marimba by Christine Hélot, Patricia Velasco, Antun Kojton

Our books are available on our website and on all major online bookstores as paperback and e-book. Some of our books have been translated in over a dozen languages. For a listing of all books published by TBR Books, information on our series, or for our submission guidelines for authors, visit our website at:

www.tbr-books.org

CaleC
▬▬▬▬▬ ▬▬ ▬ ▪▪

About CALEC

The Center for the Advancement of Languages, Education, and Communities (CALEC) is a nonprofit organization focused on promoting multilingualism, empowering multilingual families, and fostering cross-cultural understanding. The Center's mission is in alignment with the United Nations' Sustainable Development Goals. Our mission is to establish language as a critical life skill, by developing and implementing bilingual education programs, promoting diversity, reducing inequality, and helping to provide quality education. Our programs seek to protect world cultural heritage and support teachers, authors, and families by providing the knowledge and resources to create vibrant multilingual communities.

The specific objectives and purpose of our organization are:

- To develop and implement education programs that promote multilingualism and cross-cultural understanding, and establish an inclusive and equitable quality education, including internship and leadership training. [SDG # 4, Quality Education]

- To publish and distribute resources, including research papers, books, and case studies that seek to empower and promote the social, economic, and political inclusion of all, with a focus on language education and cultural diversity, equity, and inclusion. [SDG # 10, Reduced Inequalities]

- To help build sustainable cities and communities and support teachers, authors, researchers, and families in the advancement of multilingualism and cross-cultural understanding through collaborative tools for linguistic communities. [SDG # 11, Sustainable Cities and Communities]

- To foster strong global partnerships and cooperation, and mobilize resources across borders, to participate in events and activities that promote language education through knowledge sharing and coaching, empowering parents, and teachers, and building multilingual societies. [SDG # 17, Partnerships for the Goals]

SOME GOOD REASONS TO SUPPORT US

Your donation helps:

- develop our publishing and translation activities so that more languages are represented.

- provide access to our online book platform to daycare centers, schools, and cultural centers in underserved areas.

- support local and sustainable action in favor of education and multilingualism.

- implement projects that advance dual-language education

- organize workshops for parents, conferences with large audiences, meet-the-author chats, and talks with experts in multilingualism.

DONATE ONLINE

For all your questions, contact our team by email at contact@calec.org or donate online on our website:

www.calec.org

www.ingramcontent.com/pod-product-compliance
Lightning Source LLC
Chambersburg PA
CBHW021233090426
42740CB00006B/513